Cover art by Jose Razo.
Illustrations by Loren Rodriguez.

Front Cover: *"Jesus in the Eye of the Storm"* portrays the saving grace of Jesus reaching out to us in our darkest moments of despair. *If thou shalt confess with thy mouth the Lord Jesus, and shalt believe in thine heart that God hath raised him from the dead, thou shalt be saved.* (Romans 10:9). The painting is full of symbols that point to the Savior like *the Sun of Righteousness*. (Malachi 4:2). See if you can find them.

Inside Cover: *Angels* announced the *miracle birth* of the *Deliverer of Israel*. He was *sold out* for silver and He was led like a lamb to the slaughter, yet His was *innocent blood.* They blinded Him and took Him and stretched out his arms as a Great Sacrifice. Who is this Greatest of Sacrifices? *Be not affrighted: Ye seek Jesus of Nazareth, which was crucified: he is risen…* (Mark 16:6).

ISBN: 978-1-952229-00-8

Sword Bearers Ministries
PO Box 2010 Richland, Washington

PREFACE AND DEDICATION

Theories of evolution and the origin of the universe lead many, mainly scientists like myself, to believe that Creation is nothing but an accidental sequence of events that ultimately can be explained by natural laws. I was skeptical of the existence of God, and I tried to disprove His existence. The incomprehensible expanse of our Universe seems to render our existence inconsequential. Few scientists truly believe in God or His promise of an eternal life. Many see God as a cruel figment of our imagination. Some have even taken their lives because they see no purpose in living; they have no hope. We've watched as those around us succumb to aging, cancer, heart disease, suicide, murder, and accidental death. We've watched as hurricanes, tornadoes, tsunamis, earthquakes, and fires, destroy lives and the environment. Why believe in a God that would allow these things to happen? Are we living a *God Delusion*? The Scriptures speak of the invasion of our world by the prince of darkness and his legions of fallen angels. Are we to believe that this dark prince has stolen Earth as his kingdom of sin and death? Yet we are told that the *Prince of Light* will take back His Kingdom and provide a way of escape from sin and the grave. This all seemed too incredible, until I discovered the *Guardians: Keepers of God's Secret Code*. But why has this evidence been kept secret since the foundation? How could multiple authors, hundreds of years apart, predict the future so consistently and accurately? The Code provides undeniable evidence of a Supernatural Author.

My beloved wife spent many a restless night pointing and guiding me in the Way of Truth. Without her encouragement, this book would never have been written and I would have missed out on eternal life. This book is dedicated to my wife, my mom and dad, my siblings, my family, my son, my daughters, my grandchildren, my friends and co-workers, the scientific community, unbelievers, doubters, my church family, my bible students, artists, and editors that they may have the confidence and comfort that the God of Israel exists.

Table of Contents

He that sits above the wheels of the heavenly chariot still guides the affairs of mankind[1]

In the context of the vastness of space and the immensity of time we are as nothing. Why would anyone care?

Soon there will be Time no Longer![2]
Is God in control of your destiny?

---

[1] Ezekiel 10:1-4; Ezekiel 1:4-28.
[2] Revelation 10:6.

Prologue: Mysterious Secret of the Holy Grail

Knowing this first, that there shall come in the last days scoffers, walking after their own lusts, And saying, Where is the promise of his coming? for since the fathers fell asleep, all things continue as [they were] from the beginning of the creation. For this they willingly are ignorant of, that by the word of God the heavens were of old, and the earth standing out of the water and in the water: Whereby the world that then was, being overflowed with water, perished...[3]

Sin is an insidious thing. It doth like a cancer grow within the body and deep within the mind and soul, destroying the regal being that we are meant to be. It dulls our mind, weakens our body, and blinds our senses that we ***seeing see not, and hearing hear not, neither do we understand***.[4] It is more infectious than any virus or flu, spreading across the world with far more devastating consequences than any other known contagion. None can shed its grasp, none rich or poor, young or old, can escape its consequences. For the ***wages of sin are death***.[5] For ceaseless ages man has sought antidotes but none can be produced, none can be purchased, there is no way of escape save **One**.

Scientists in my field are trained that the earth is billions of years old. As a practicing geochemist, I was trained to believe in the gradual evolution of our universe, our planet, and life. We accept these principles as guiding truths and as the anchors of our research. And in many respects, I still do. So how can we, how can I, accept the Bible as the Word of God? I became increasingly skeptical of the existence of God. So I set forth to free my wife

---

[3] 2 Peter 3:3-6.
[4] Matthew 13:13-14.
[5] Romans 6:23.

and others of this "***God Delusion***."[6] My approach was to use scientific methods to prove that the Bible was simply a compilation by men.[7] After all, the Scriptures claim that they are written by the guidance of the Spirit.[8] And Christ Himself boldly claims that the Old Testament Scriptures are about Himself.[9] How could they be about Him? So I began a decades long cross-examination of His claims to debunk the notion of the existence of God.

But an incredible discovery of a mysterious Old Testament encryption changes the way that I view our Universe, the existence of God, and the Savior of mankind. It was as if the veil had been lifted from my eyes.[10] What I uncovered were enumerable systematically embedded events in the lives of Old and New Testament Guardians whose lives are deliberately choreographed, positively linking those of the Old with those of the New as if by supernatural DNA. During my journey, I unearthed many other fingerprints of God, including patterns of the heavenly sanctuary, literary light waves, and the spiral-form literary structure that starts in Genesis and is completed in Revelation.

Numerous others have discovered codes and structures throughout the Scriptures that are deliberately incorporated into the text. Sir Isaac Newton's studies led him to symbolic patterns in the Torah. And he found many such codes more than 250 years earlier the discovery of numerical codes of Drosnin[11] and Witzum, Rips, and Rosenberg.[12] Amazingly, Sir Isaac Newton discovered strange symbolic Bible codes in the Old Testament in an effort similar to mine. Of course, Newton had to master Hebrew to crack these codes! Many have found that the four letters of the Hebrew word (תּוֹרָה), translated as TORAH in English, occur at a 50 letter

---

[6] Richard Dawkins, *The God Delusion*, Black Swan, 2007, pp. 294.

[7] 1 Timothy 6:20, 21.

[8] 1 Peter 1:11; 2 Peter 1:21; Ephesians 3:5.

[9] Luke 24:27, 44.

[10] 2 Corinthians 3:13-18.

[11] Michael Drosnin, *The Bible Code* (New York: Simon & Schuster, 1997), 179p.

[12] Witzum, D., Rips, E. and Rosenberg, Y. 1994. Equidistant Letter Sequences in the Book of Genesis. Statistical Sci., Volume 9, Number 3, 429-438.

count interval starting in Genesis and ending in the middle of the Book of Leviticus, without a computer. Searchers later realized that the word for TORAH was spelled backwards from the center of Leviticus to the end of Deuteronomy.

What took Weissmandl[13] intense concentration and study, can now be mastered by Bible code software of equidistant letter spacing (ELS). Is this literary fabric the signature of God or just an ancient writing style? Newton thought it was the signature of God, and so do some of the modern Bible code researchers. Or was it a style that Moses learned in the Pharaoh's court? Or is this "code" simply a statistical oddity? The image below shows the Hebrew four letter word for "Torah" at a 50 letter interval.[14]

After years of research Drosnin, was still an atheist. He concluded that "there was a code, but not proof there was a God." The view of many other modern scholars is that the number code in the structure of the Torah is adapted as a compositional style for structuring the text by the ancient scribes. Who's right?

It appears that the biblical text was composed according to preconceived models and patterns shaped by certain numbers that regulate the amount of words, sentences, and verses. Specific numbers were used to forge the structure of the text in its different component parts. Like musical compositions, which are artistically constructed and arranged with the help

---

[13] Witzum and others. 1994. IBID.
[14] Bible Code in Genesis 1:1-4. 1909 . Public domain.

of rhythm and melody, so literary texts in biblical antiquity were composed and structurally organized with the help of certain numbers...writing...seems to have involved compositional techniques inextricably bound up with counting.[15]

Could the creation of the Scriptures have been guided by an unseen Hand? Newton thought so. So do I. But the proof of God's existence requires far more than equidistant letter spacing which appears to be the work of men. In my opinion Newton's discoveries of the Bible went far beyond equidistant letter spacing. He wrote a treatise on the **prophetic books of Daniel and Revelation**. According to Newton,[16] although Daniel lived in the time of Babylon, the prophecies given to Daniel by the angel Gabriel accurately record the rise and fall of kingdoms, hundreds of years into the future. Newton's discovery of symbolic and prophetic language convinced me that the Bible is no ordinary book. Consider the following symbolic language:

The ram which thou sawest having [two] horns [are] the kings of Media and Persia and the rough goat [is] the king of Grecia...[17]

Newton realized that the Biblical characters are symbols. That was an important key to me. If scientists like Newton and Einstein maintained a deep interest in the Bible for decades, then the Bible is no ordinary book. How could anyone accurately predict the rise and fall of future kingdoms without supernatural eyes? How could anyone read the dreams of another without supernatural help?[18] Once I reviewed Newton's discoveries, I decided I'd better investigate further! And Newton made estimates of the time of the return of Christ! After all, Newton is credited with the development of integral calculus.

---

[15] Labuschagne, C.J. *Numerical Secrets of the Bible: Rediscovering the Bible Codes*. (2000). Bibal Press, N. Richland Hills, TX. Page 1 of 192 pages.
[16] Newton, Isaac, Sir. Daniel and the Apocalypse. J. Murray London. 1922.
[17] Daniel 8:20, 21.
[18] Daniel 2:19-49.

The Secret Golden Key

The Secret Golden Key unlocks the evidence that proves that God exists. By properly applying the key, one discovers a hidden world behind the lines of the sacred Scriptures. The Old Testament Scriptures are like a modern cryptogram commonly referred to by the Secret Agencies as a picture steganogram.[19] More specifically, they would be classified as a parable or a literary cyphertext.

> *The Purloined Letter is thus the extreme example of steganography as a message that is not what and where it seems to be. So it is ... of steganography in general, that they show things in plain sight while hiding them at the same time. Professional steganographers call that which is publicly visible the "plaintext" or "payload" (which can be a painting, a piece of writing, an audio recording or any other medium) and the message hidden in it, the "cyphertext", "covert message," or "package"[20]*

The art of the parable is a brain tease, designed to maintain your attention for days, months, even years. It could even be used to mesmerize you. Riddles and parables[21] are literary means of captivating and maintaining your attention by setting forth a fascinating puzzle as the plaintext which hides a deeper meaning. Why? Because, the riddle sets *a nail in a sure place.*[22] Some parables are meant to be easily understood and others are meant to be hidden and kept secret except from the most diligent of seekers. Jesus kept secrets veiled as parables so His Plan would succeed.

> *All these things spake Jesus unto the multitude in parables; and without a parable spake he not unto them: That it might be fulfilled which was spoken by the*

---

[19] The art or practice of concealing a message, image, or file within another message, image, or file.

[20] Florian Cramer. February 2017. Hiding in Plain Sight: Amy Suo Wu's The Kadinsky Collective, Aksioma Institute for Contemporary Art. Slovenia.

[21] Matthew 13:34.

[22] Isaiah 22:23.

prophet, saying, I will open my mouth in parables; I will utter things which have been kept secret from the foundation of the world.[23]

Unbeknownst to the Scribes and Pharisees, each event, step-by-step, in the life of Jesus unlocks secrets of the Old Testament. Each event is the fulfillment of multiple hidden prophecies concerning Himself. Even the Exodus walk of Moses and Israel are given to us as plaintext events behind which messages disclose end-time events yet to come.

Now all these things happened unto them for ensamples: and they are written for our admonition, upon whom the ends of the world are come.[24]

Far greater than all the revelations ever opened to mankind, is this one single Secret Golden Key that is revealed in this Book. And this Secret Golden Key opens the Lock that some men have referred to as the Holy Grail that opens the Door to Eternal Life. And within this *Golden Cup* is a way of escape from sin and death. With it, we can walk out of the darkness that clouds our minds and weakens our bodies.

Yet fundamentally, this mysterious Golden Key is designed to be understood by children, like those in my Bible Studies: Shannon, Christopher, Omar, Elvin, Hasiel, and so many others.

---

[23] Matthew 13:34, 35.
[24] 1 Corinthians 1:11.

CROSS-EXAMINATION

Search the scriptures; ... they are they which testify of me. [25] Ask, and it shall be given you; seek, and ye shall find; knock, and it shall be opened unto you: For every one that asketh receiveth; and he that seeketh findeth; and to him that knocketh it shall be opened.[26]

Examining the supernatural realm with scientific methods was my gospel for seeking truth. I'm a skeptic. No *"leap of faith"* for me. I need tangible, reproducible evidence. How about you? Science has taught me to be skeptical and objective. For more than a decade I conducted systematic scientific studies of the Old Testament, and today I stand armed with overwhelming evidence, unlocked by the Secret Golden Key, to make the case for God. Instead of disproving God, God soon proved to me that He's alive. **Why believe in God? Why believe in the Bible? Why believe in the realm of the supernatural and life after death?** Why? Because the Scriptures hide the evidence of an encrypted message in plain sight! Is there a Golden Key to unlock the cipher lock?

---

[25] John 5:39.
[26] Matthew 7:7, 8.

1 *Skeptic in Search of the Secret Golden Keys*

Now to him that is of power to stablish you according to my gospel, and the preaching of Jesus Christ, according to the revelation of the mystery, <u>which was kept secret since the world began</u>, But now is made manifest, and by the scriptures of the prophets[27]

For the scientist in me, the most intriguing, awe-inspiring, and yet most inconceivable passages found in the writings of the Gospels of Matthew, Mark, Luke, and John, and the entire Bible for that matter, are those that point to the supernatural. Creation by an unseen God, the healing miracles of Christ, a world-wide flood, the resurrection of Lazarus and Jesus, and the promise of eternal life for believers, all seemed to be unsupportable. Science must develop its hypotheses, theories, and fact based upon tangible, testable, reproducible evidence. How do you test the supernatural? Conversely, theologians claim that the existence of God and the supernatural occurrences of the Scriptures require a leap of faith. But none of this "*leap of faith*" for me. I'm a skeptic. I need tangible, reproducible evidence. Examining the supernatural realm with scientific methods was my gospel for seeking truth. And that's what I sought; the Truth!

A monumental study was in order. Emotion had to be set aside. The evidence must provide the verdict. Science has taught me to be skeptical and objective. After all, in scientific circles, the discussion of religion is virtually taboo. For more than a decade I conducted systematic scientific studies of the Old Testament, and today I stand armed with overwhelming evidence, unlocked by the Secret Golden Key, to make the case for God. Instead of disproving God, God soon proved to me that He's alive.

---

[27] Romans 16:25, 26.

Little Black Book

In the summer of 2002, my family and I had travelled by train, from Washington State to upstate New York, to visit my parents on the North shore of Oneida Lake. The homestead, nestled on the lakefront, had been owned by my grandparents and was built in the late 1700s. The walls of the two story home had been raised by a team of horses. The original maple trees that grew in the front of the house were cut down by my cousins and they measured the diameters of the stumps at more than six feet across. It was a place full of fond memories. My parents had turned the place into a bed and breakfast and they assigned us the front upstairs room where my grandparents once slept. It was evening in the early summer and you could see the lights of the suburbs of Syracuse twinkling on the distant lake shore about seven miles away. It was the place where I had learned how to swim. It was the place where my siblings gathered with their children and we sailed on dad's Hobie Cat, paddled his canoes, and water-skied. Suffice it to say it was a place where we could all sit back and relax at the foot of nature.

The bedroom had an old brass bed, two windows overlooking the lake, and memorabilia and pictures of my grandparents. We opened the windows to allow the summer breeze to circulate in the room and turned into bed. We could hear the fish jumping and geese squabbling in the distance. I was home! As I was settling in, I noticed a little black book on the end table. On the cover, the book read "New Testament" with the subtitle "Old Testament Prophecy Edition."[28] It reminded me that my siblings and I regularly attended the Methodist churches that were in the little towns all along the North Shore of the lake. But it was my education as a scientist that took me away from my childhood Christian training, at least for a season.[29]

As I opened the cover to the book, it was as if I fell into the world of the Supernatural. For in that little Black Book, a love story

---

[28]Amazon, King James. Publisher: Million Testament Campaigns. 1982. 647pp.
[29] Proverbs 22:6.

unfolded before me like none I had ever seen or heard before. And it was set in the midst of a galactic war. Could it be true?

Angel Wars

<u>According to the Scriptures,</u> **in the beginning, God created the heaven and the earth.**[30] The angels watched in delight as Jesus, the Son of God, also known as the WORD, created[31] the heavens and the worlds of the Universe.[32] He stretched out the Universe like a garment[33] defying our understanding of the physics and chemistry of time, space, and matter. And by stretching[34] out the visible and dark matter, space, and time, He set a Universe in place[35] that was mere moments old from edge to edge. Yet the time it would take for a newly generated ray of light to traverse the width of the Universe would be on the order of 50 billion years. And He set His crowning jewel in the midst of our Milky Way galaxy; a place we call Earth. And it was through the One called Jesus,[36] that the Trinity created man and woman in the image of God[37] and set them in the midst of a garden, east of Eden. **And on the seventh day God ended his work which he had made; and he rested on the seventh day from all his work which he had made. And God blessed the seventh day, and sanctified it: because that in it he had rested from all his work which God created and made.**[38]

We are told that, in the awe and beauty of this Creation, a trusted angel and confidant fell to the grasp of sin. He was Lucifer, the

---

[30] Genesis 1:1.
[31] John 1:3.
[32] John 1:1-4. Hebrews 1:2.
[33] Psalm 104:2; Isaiah 40:22.
[34] Psalm 104:2; 136:6; Isaiah 40:22; 42:5; 45:12; (Qur'an, Suras 51:47-48).
[35] Explaining the fine-tuned constants of the universe; e.g., cosmological constant, the omega density parameter, and many others.
[36] John 1:3.
[37] Genesis 1:26, 27.
[38] Genesis 2:2, 3.

anointed cherub[39] that stood by the very throne of the Trinity. Lucifer's ego was crushed and he became insanely jealous when he overheard God the Father say to the Son, *Let us make man in our image, after our likeness...*[40] Lucifer was jealous that he was being left out of something so amazing. Lucifer, now referred to as Satan,[41] soon conspired to take the throne.[42] Through devious means, Satan assembled an army of sympathizers and admirers among the angelic hosts through political means by persuading them that he was most worthy to run the government of this new Creation. The angels were easily deceived by his every word and they were persuaded of his proposal, for they were not the least suspicious. **After all, they had never heard a lie before.**

We are informed that Satan's followers must have been so deceived that they believed his lies and they gave their steadfast allegiance to him. And in so doing, they broke the commandments that were the very reflection of God's character. By taking their eyes from the throne, and looking upon Satan as their leader, they praised Satan as their god. It was then that I could almost hear the WORDs of God coming from the throne saying, *Thou shalt have no other gods before me.*[43] *Thou shalt not bear false witness.. Thou shalt not covet...*[44] And in the end, Satan and his followers were found guilty of breaking all of God's LAW for *whosoever shall keep the whole law, and yet offend in one [point], he is guilty of all.*[45] The entire government of God had come into question and was in danger of being toppled. The Trinity knew that the Seat of God was in danger of being overthrown, but not in the classical sense of war and bloodshed. The word "war" in the Greek (polemos) means contention, controversy, or argument. It is the root of the word "politics." The very character of God was

---

[39] Isaiah 14:12-15; Ezekiel 28:14-18.

[40] Genesis 1:27.

[41] The change in name from "Lucifer" to "Satan" is a key to our study. The change of name represents his change in character. "Lucifer," meaning bearer of Light, became "Satan" the adversary, accuser, and the devil.

[42] Isaiah 14:12-15; Ezekiel 28:13-18.

[43] Exodus 20:3.

[44] Exodus 20:16, 17.

[45] James 2:10.

expressed in His governance and His Law and it was through trust and love that the angels delighted in doing His pleasure. Heaven's government was founded on this yoke[46] of LOVE.

If this were all true, then these immortal beings had broken the LAW of God because they had questioned His authority. In essence, they placed another "god" above God the Father and the Son because, in backing Satan, they placed Satan's word above God's WORD. And in doing so, they had sinned because *sin is the transgression of the LAW.*[47] And because they sinned, *the wages of sin is death.*[48] They had unwittingly sealed their own fate: these immortals would die the same death that they brought to mortal man… but they have no Savior. Satan does not have the power to save and his sacrifice would not be worthy.

We are told that sometime following the Creation of the world, Lucifer began to openly challenge God and *there was war in heaven: Michael and his angels fought against the dragon; and the dragon fought and his angels, and prevailed not; neither was their place found any more in heaven. And the great dragon was cast out, that old serpent, called the Devil, and Satan, which deceiveth the whole world: he was cast out into the earth, and his angels were cast out with him.*[49] Satan, and those he deceived, were exiled because they threatened the very government of Heaven. They were exiled to Earth to contain the spread of the contagion of sin.

Once Satan, and his fallen angels were exiled to Earth he continued to use his same tactics of lies and innuendos to take dominion over the Earth; dominion that had been conferred upon Adam. And when Adam and Eve were ensnared and had fallen to sin, the Secret Plan that had been established by the Trinity was unleashed. War was declared between Satan and the Seed of the woman.[50] But Satan had stolen dominion over the Earth. And he would do

---

[46] Matthew 11:30.
[47] 1 John 3:4.
[48] Romans 6:23.
[49] Revelation 12:7-9.
[50] Genesis 3:15.

everything possible to destroy the Seed of the woman in his attempt to keep the Creator, the one we call Jesus, from taking back planet Earth.

As I continued to study Satan and his objectives, I realized that his diabolical mind reasoned that if God pardoned Adam and Eve, He would have to pardon Satan and his fallen angels out of His character of fairness and love. But *if the Godhead pardoned Adam and Eve, but did not pardon Satan and the fallen angels, Satan would claim that the Godhead did not govern impartially. Then Satan could claim that God is not LOVE and topple the government of God.* But *God is LOVE;*[51] therefore, the Godhead had no choice but to implement the crucifixion of Jesus as the key to the secret of the Plan of Salvation.

The war would be a series of legal battles or "mind games" witnessed by heaven. To be sure, these mind games led to viciousness, violence, and wickedness upon men. All of heaven watched in wonderment, as the war between Christ and Satan unfolded before the Highest Court in the Universe. From the beginning, Satan unfolded his testimony with lies and deceit. He thought sure that his unfair tactics would give him an advantage, knowing that the Trinity was constrained to their LAW of LOVE. Yet his approach was not always successful. In the wilderness, Satan deliberately misquoted Scripture to cause Jesus to fall to sin. But *Jesus quoted Scripture as the antivenom.* And Jesus won the 40-day battle of WORDs. Truth and Love overcame lies and hate.

Satan's opposition to the throne soon led to judgment from the Highest of Courts. *And I beheld till the thrones were cast down, and the Ancient of days did sit, whose garment [was] white as snow, and the hair of his head like the pure wool: his throne [was like] the fiery flame, [and] his wheels [as] burning fire. A fiery stream issued and came forth from before him: thousand thousands ministered unto him, and ten thousand times ten thousand stood before him: the judgment was set, and the books*

---

[51] 1 John 4:8, 16.

were opened.[52]   With this incredible story of angel wars and the opening of the Court of Heaven as a backdrop, I began to review the Bible with my scientific eyes. The Biblical account seemed too far-fetched to be believable.   I was confident I would soon accumulate a mountain of evidence to discredit it. My approach was to find inconsistencies in the underlying logic; not trivial issues but incongruencies of logic.

Apostle Conspiracy?

One night I re-opened the Little Black Book to the passages recorded by the Apostle Matthew, and I was soon through his short 28 chapters. For the entire week, I spent time tracing the sources of his writing, and I realized that Matthew's primary objective was to prove that Jesus was the Messiah. He unfolds his case by testifying that the life events of Jesus fulfilled prophecies that were recorded in the Old Testament, written hundreds of years earlier. His approach was fascinating and it would prove to be the key that I was looking for to open the treasure of God's Secret Code. I wondered why Matthew was so careful to connect Old Testament prophecies to the life events of Jesus.   What were Matthew's motives?

My mind was soon captivated, as it wrestled with the account of Matthew. I soon realized that Matthew wasn't present with Jesus until long after many of the prophecies about the Messiah were fulfilled.   Half of Matthew's prophecies, that he declares to be **"fulfilled"**,[53] were events that occurred long before Matthew even met this Jesus. Yet he documents the birth of Christ as if he were there. I refer you to Matthew's own writings, chapter 9, verse 9.[54] This observation seemed to limit Matthew's testimony.   Much of Matthew's evidence was second-hand or hear-say. It appears to be circumstantial and to cast doubt on all of his testimony. The same is true for the written testimonies of the other Gospel witnesses.

---

[52] Daniel 7:9,10.
[53] See for example, Matthew 1:22,23; 2:15; 2:17; 2:23; 4:14-16; and 8:17.
[54] Matthew 9:9.

Mark wasn't even among the original apostles. From what has been ascertained, much of Mark's work is based on second hand information, gathered from others, yet his testimony was the first of the four Gospel accounts to be written down! But a little research shows that much of John Mark's writings were dictated to him by the Apostle Peter. Therefore, it could be considered first, and not second-hand information! After all, Mark was Peter's interpreter.[55] And if one were to do only a limited amount of homework and due diligence, one could be led to believe that much of their writings aren't even eye-witness accounts. Some might conclude that there was even a CONSPIRACY instigated by Jesus, Himself! But that hypothesis was quickly dashed.

Cowards become Martyrs

After the resurrection, the once cowardly apostles seemed to become courageous overnight. Why? Not just one, but all of the apostles became fearless, and most died from horrific causes. Tradition tells us that Matthew accompanied Andrew to Syria where he was burned to death.[56] Even the apostle Peter was crucified upside down at his own request, not feeling worthy of being crucified in an upright position like his Lord. Recognition of the cruel deaths that the apostles allowed themselves to be subjected to, convinced me that there had to be more to the story. But what could it be? Had there really been a resurrection? And if

---

[55] Papias of Hierapolis (A.D. 60-130) *"And the presbyter said this. Mark having become the interpreter of Peter, wrote down accurately whatsoever he remembered. It was not, however, in exact order that he related the sayings or deeds of Christ. For he neither heard the Lord nor accompanied Him. But afterwards, as I said, he accompanied Peter, who accommodated his instructions to the necessities [of his hearers], but with no intention of giving a regular narrative of the Lord's sayings. Wherefore Mark made no mistake in thus writing some things as he remembered them. For of one thing he took especial care, not to omit anything he had heard, and not to put anything fictitious into the statements."[4]*

[56] Fox's Book of Martyrs Or a History of the Lives, Sufferings, and Triumphant Deaths of the Primitive Protestant Martyrs. John Foxe. EBook #22400, English. ISO-8859-1.

so, what had they learned after the resurrection? I concluded that the examination of the writings of Matthew alone was insufficient evidence to prove or disprove the existence of God, at least from a scientific perspective. I was still searching.

"Fulfilled" Keys

I soon realized, that Matthew's use of the Old Testament patterns are a seed of an idea which germinates, grows, and evolves into a plant that bears fruit. That is, the immature thought set forth in the Old Testament is brought to maturity through Jesus and His Plan of Salvation. We'll find that this understanding is key to numerous applications. It provides a glimmer of **the Secret Golden Key that the Apostles were given to unlock the text** after the resurrection of Jesus. You could say their eyes were opened.[57]

> *This same re-echoing of Israel's past experiences is at work in the other **fulfillment passages**... Matthew's **fulfillment passages** provide an excellent example of how the scriptures of ancient Israel were being read in the earliest churches. **The Jewish believers in [Jesus]** the Crucified-and-Raised One **read their scriptures with new eyes**. By interpreting those texts **through the lens of their resurrection faith in Jesus**, new meanings and applications developed that had not arisen before.[58]*

After nearly two decades of intense research, it has become evident that the mysterious codification of the Scriptures provides its own basis of validation. This codification is internally consistent, congruent, and complementary among numerous authors, separated by hundreds, even thousands of years. As you'll soon realize, the unseen Author designed the encryptions, as **hidden evidence** that has been kept *secret since the foundation of the*

---

[57] Luke 24:45.
[58] Boston College December 13, 2016.
https://www.bc.edu/...matthewsinfancynarrative/matthews_fulfillmentpassages.html

world.[59] But why has it been secretly hidden? Within the code are *treasures of darkness, and hidden riches of secret places* that we may know that God exists.[60]

The ancient code reveals that the world has been in the vice of supernatural warfare since shortly after its Creation.[61] The mysterious code is so simple in concept that it can be understood by children yet *for many, their minds are blinded: for until this day remaineth the same veil untaken away in the reading of the Old Testament; which [veil] is done away in Christ. But even unto this day, when Moses is read, the veil is upon their heart. Nevertheless when it shall turn to the Lord, the veil shall be taken away.*[62]

Why believe in God? Why believe in the Bible? Why believe in the realm of the supernatural and life after death? Why? Because the Scriptures hide the evidence of an encrypted message in plain sight!

---

[59] Matthew 13:35.
[60] Isaiah 45:3.
[61] Revelation 12:7.
[62] 2 Corinthians 3:14-16.

2   *They Testify of Me!*

These [are] the words which I spake unto you, while I was yet with you, that all things must be fulfilled, which were written in the law of Moses, and [in] the prophets, and [in] the psalms, concerning me. <u>*Then opened he their understanding*</u>*, that they might understand the scriptures, And said unto them, Thus it is written, and thus it behoved Christ to suffer, and to rise from the dead the third day.*[63] *To him give all the prophets witness, that through his name whosoever believeth in him shall receive remission of sins.*[64]

Jesus made bold statements, that the writings of the Old Testament testify of Himself. I immediately saw these statements as the basis for cross-examining the Bible. From my perspective, either the ancient writings testify of Jesus or they don't. Jesus set forth a challenge for the people in His day[65] saying, *Search the scriptures… they are they which testify of me.*[66] And later He said, *Before Abraham was, I AM. Then took they up stones to cast at him: but Jesus hid himself, and went out of the temple, going through the midst of them, and so passed by.*[67]

The scribes and Pharisees didn't believe that Jesus was the pre-existent Son of God. After all, they knew Him as the lowly son of a carpenter. *Can there any good thing come out of Nazareth?*[68] They made the assumption that their Messiah would appear as a King, surrounded with all the trappings of royalty. They made a

---

[63] Luke 24:44-46;
[64] Acts 10:43.
[65] John 5:39.
[66] John 5:39.
[67] John 8:58, 59.
[68] John 1:46.

fundamental mistake in their assumption, confusing the imagery of the Second Coming of Jesus with His First Coming. Their misassumption only explained selected portions of the Old Testament texts. It left many important passages of His First Coming unaddressed; especially passages that spoke of His death, burial, and resurrection. Passages like Isaiah Chapter 53, Psalm 22, and Jonah's Chapter 1 should have given them pause to rethink their paradigm. Any interpretation of the ancient Scriptures must be inclusive of all passages. **If the Scriptures are truly guided by a Supernatural Being, then all portions must be consistent**.

Because of the misassumption of the scribes and Pharisees, they were sure that Jesus was a blasphemer and deserved to be stoned to death. But why didn't they carefully interrogate the Scriptures to see if Jesus met the test of the Messiah? The religious scholars certainly knew of the Messianic prophecies. When Herod asked them where He would be born, *they said unto him, In Bethlehem of Judaea: for thus it is written by the prophet...*[69] The wise men of Herod's court knew where the Messiah would be born and they knew about other Messianic prophecies, even when He would be born![70] *Then Herod, when he saw that he was mocked of the wise men [Magi of the east], was exceeding wroth, and sent forth, and slew all the children that were in Bethlehem, and in all the coasts thereof, from two years old and under, according to the time which he had diligently inquired of the wise men.*[71] But who really provoked Herod? Were there supernatural forces at work?

So with careful consideration I set forth to prove or disprove these claims of Jesus. If the religious leaders dismissed Jesus as the Messiah, why should we believe? On the other hand, how did the Magi know about the birth of the Messiah? How did they know it was His star?[72] What evidence would we need to find in the sacred text that would prove that Jesus is the Messiah? I was hopeful that the statements made by Jesus were testable and that the results of

---

[69] Matthew 2:5, 6.
[70] Daniel 9:26.
[71] Matthew 2:16.
[72] Numbers 24:17; Matthew 2:2.

the tests could be independently verified. On the surface, His claims seemed exaggerated, but I hoped they would lead to the evidence that I was seeking. Upon Jesus' boldest claims rest the credibility of the New Testament, the Messiahship of Jesus, the existence of God, and the existence of the supernatural.[73]

They Testify of Me

Luke's testimony bears two records of the **CENTRAL BOLD CLAIM** made by Jesus. After the resurrection, on the road to Emmaus, Jesus conversed with two confused travelers. They were on their way home from the Passover feast. As they travelled along the dark and rugged road, they grieved and were disheartened. Then Jesus mysteriously appeared as a stranger in their midst, and began to converse with them. And they said to Jesus, *we trusted that it had been he which should have redeemed Israel: and beside all this, to day is the third day since these things were done. Yea, and certain women also of our company made us astonished, which were early at the sepulchre; And when they found not his body, they came, saying, that they had also seen a vision of angels, which said that he was alive. And certain of them which were with us went to the sepulchre, and found [it] even so as the women had said: but him they saw not.*

These follower's had watched as Jesus died a gruesome, bloody, and terrifying death on the Cross. They were traumatized. Because that imagery painfully seared their minds; they gave up their belief that He would be resurrected on the third day. His followers had given Him up for dead! They didn't even believe the women that reportedly saw angels and saw the empty tomb. They thought the women imagined what they saw. Because of their disbelief, Jesus was deeply discouraged. *Then he said unto them, O fools, and slow of heart to believe all that the prophets have spoken: Ought not Christ to have suffered these things, and to enter into his glory? And beginning at Moses and all the prophets, he expounded unto them in all the scriptures the things*

---

[73] 1 Peter 1:11; 2 Peter 1:21; Ephesians 3:3-5.

<u>*concerning himself.*</u>[74] If Jesus was truly legitimate, He must have been greatly discouraged that the apostles and disciples still doubted, especially with all of His miracles and teachings.

On a second occasion, in the Upper Room Jesus said, *These [are] the words which I spake unto you, while I was yet with you, that <u>all things must be fulfilled, which were written in the law of Moses, and [in] the prophets, and [in] the psalms, concerning me.</u> Then <u>opened he their understanding,</u> that they might understand the scriptures...*[75] What was it that finally changed their minds? Why was it only after Jesus appeared to His apostles and disciples and proved that He fulfilled the Scriptures, that they finally believed? What did Jesus show them that was so convincing? We are told that it was through the Old Testament Scriptures that Jesus opened their understanding. What did Jesus show them in the Old Testament that was so convincing? What evidence would it take for those of our day to believe? Could we open the same information that had been kept secret?

Peter, Stephen, and Paul preached that Christ was the fulfillment of the prophecies recorded by Moses, in the writings of the prophets, and in the psalms. Several years after the resurrection, Paul likewise testified of the mystery of the Scriptures that are now unlocked saying, *How that by revelation he made known unto me the mystery; (as I wrote afore in few words, Whereby, when ye read, ye may understand my knowledge in the mystery of Christ) Which in other ages was not made known unto the sons of men, as it is now revealed unto his holy apostles and prophets by the Spirit...*[76] And Paul <u>*expounded and testified the kingdom of God, persuading them concerning Jesus, both out of the law of Moses, and [out of] the prophets, from morning till evening.*</u>[77] Paul was a learned scholar and would not have been readily fooled. So once again, I realized that there was likely more to the story. After all, why would Paul, Peter, and Stephen use the law of Moses and the

---

[74] Luke 24:13-27
[75] Luke 24:44, 45
[76] Ephesians 3:3-5.
[77] Acts 28:23.

prophets to testify of Jesus? My conclusion is that Jesus opened their understanding[78] of the Scriptures.

But how could the Old Testament testify of Jesus? There had to be more to the Old Testament evidence than the Messianic prophecies.

Event Sequence Timeline

It seemed as if Matthew's summation of the life of Jesus was a deposition in a Court case. His deposition is given on behalf of Jesus, but what was Matthew's motivation? Matthew's writings provide an event sequence from the birth of Jesus to His ascension from the Mount of Olives. Like a detective or an attorney, it is important to establish the sequence of events in a legal hearing. Detectives, lawyers, and even scientists, frequently develop detailed reconstructions of incidents, phenomena, even chemical reactions, as an event sequence analysis. Matthew's writings are not only important to us but they are a testimony in the Highest Court. I knew that if I were to break the case, I would have to develop a timeline.

Harmony of the Gospels

When the events in the writings of Matthew are pieced together with the Gospels of Mark, Luke, and John we can begin to establish a detailed timeline sequence of events. Numerous attempts have been made to show that the four Gospels tell the same story from different perspectives. Each of the four accounts represent independent views of the events in the life of Jesus written after the events occurred. Why are their testimonies considered to be in harmony with one another? Why was each so driven to document the evidence as they best knew it?

---

[78] Luke 24:44, 45.

Great Cloud of Witnesses

The War in Heaven soon became a war for the Universe. Would the Universe be governed by Christ or Satan? Satan has long argued that the Gospels are not TRUTH. But a *Great Cloud of Witnesses*[79] prove that the writings of the Old Testament *testify of [Jesus].*[80] And these witnesses *have seen and do testify that the Father sent the Son [to be] the Saviour of the world.*[81] Why has this evidence been kept secret from the foundation of the world? Why? Because *we speak the wisdom of God in a mystery, [even] the hidden [wisdom], which God ordained before the world unto our glory: Which none of the princes of this world knew: for had they known [it], they would not have crucified the Lord of glory.*[82]

Why a Hidden Encryption?

Jesus won the victory at the Cross and before His ascension into heaven, *Jesus came and spake unto [His followers], saying, All power is given unto me in heaven and in earth.*[83] And Jesus said after His ascension, *I [am] he that liveth, and was dead; and, behold, I am alive for evermore, Amen; and have the keys of hell and of death.*

The Scriptures tell us that there is a hidden message in the ancient Scriptures. Again, why was this encryption hidden? *There was war in heaven: Michael and his angels fought against the dragon; and the dragon fought and his angels*[84]*...the dragon was wroth with the woman, and went to make war with the remnant of her seed, which keep the commandments of God, and have the*

---

[79] Hebrews 12:1.
[80] John 5:39.
[81] 1 John 4:14.
[82] 1 Corinthians 2:8.
[83] Matthew 28:18-20.
[84] Revelation 12:7.

testimony of Jesus Christ.[85] And who is this woman? The woman is a symbol of all that follow Jesus. They are identified as those that *keep the commandments of God, and have the testimony of Jesus Christ.*

Why Was The Encryption Hidden?

The encryption was hidden because there was war between the Supernatural forces of Christ and Satan. Jesus hid the secret encryption until the victory had been secured at the Cross!

We speak the wisdom of God in a mystery, [even] the hidden [wisdom], which God ordained before the world unto our glory: Which none of the princes of this world knew: for had they known [it], they would not have crucified the Lord of glory.[86]

Had Satan known of this secret, he would not have allowed Jesus to be crucified! The Cross was the secret weapon. Jesus had to be crucified; it was the ultimate act of LOVE. Without it, ALL would have been lost!

---

[85] Revelation 12:17.
[86] 1 Corinthians 2:7, 8.

3 *Golden Keys (52!)*

He showed himself alive after his passion by <u>many infallible</u> <u>proofs</u>, being seen of them forty days, and speaking of the things pertaining to the kingdom of God...[87] *And he said unto them, These [are] the words which I spake unto you, while I was yet with you, that all things must be fulfilled, which were written in the law of Moses, and [in] the prophets, and [in] the psalms, concerning me. <u>Then opened he their understanding, that they</u> <u>might understand the scriptures</u>, And said unto them, Thus it is written, and thus it behoved Christ to suffer, and to rise from the dead the third day...*[88]

Within the first year of my studies, I began to see numerous patterns in the Scriptures. Many of these had been reported by other authors over the centuries. For example, I soon found that chiastic structures are commonplace throughout the Old and New Testaments. It is written that the accounts of the Old are used as *ensamples: and they are written for our admonition, upon whom the ends of the world are come.*[89] The **ensamples are patterns or prophetic models** that point to events that will be **similarly** repeated **or transformed** in the future. Jesus said, *But as the days of Noe [were], so shall also the coming of the Son of man be. For as in the days that were before the flood they were eating and drinking, marrying and giving in marriage, until the day that Noe entered into the ark, And knew not until the flood came, and took them all away; so shall also the coming of the Son of man be.*[90] As in Noah's case, other accounts of the Old Testament prophetically project to events in the future. If true, these messages are also meant as a warning for us.

---

[87] Acts 1:3.
[88] Luke 24:44-46.
[89] 1 Corinthians 10:11.
[90] Matthew 24:37-39.

School Master's Lesson's

How can a Being, outside the dimension of time, communicate with those of us constrained to the physical world? This is difficult for us to understand given our perspective and framework. Time is central to our being, providing a cycle-of-life framework for us.

Results of scientific studies are usually preceded by the methods used by the investigator to communicate the legitimacy of findings. They are intended as a basis for independent verification. Similarly, the Scriptures provide cross-examination through prophecies, figures, patterns, ensamples, parables, symbols, chiasms, shadows, Divine plays, and settings among other methods, as means of communication. **Natural events contained in the Old Testament are often deliberately transformed, into a supernatural message in the New.** It is written that *the law was our schoolmaster [to bring us] unto Christ, that we might be justified by faith. But after that faith is come, we are no longer under a schoolmaster.*[91] The Books of Genesis and Exodus include a suite of literary **ensamples used to communicate supernatural messages** from the natural dimensions of the space (length, width, depth) and time that we occupy. Many of the ancient lessons were fulfilled in the First Advent of Christ. We can look at the fulfillment of events in the life of Christ from a historical perspective. The fulfillment of prophecies about the birth, life, death, burial, and resurrection of Christ are recorded in the four Gospels. They provide one means of testing the legitimacy of the Scriptures. They also provide evidence that the remaining lessons, meant for our day, will come to pass, or not.

Chiastic Structures: Light

Chiastic structures are like sine waves that are used as a fabric and a means of organizing and emphasizing a Scriptural thought.

---

[91] Galatians 3:24, 25.

Creation
Man Sins
Wicked Destroyed

Rainbow in Clouds
Song of Moses
Plagues
Trumpets

Seals
Moon as Blood

4 Horses
Cross

30 pieces Silver

Elijah

Christ's Birth

Elijah
30 pieces Silver

Cross

4 Horses

Moon as Blood

Seals
Trumpets
Plagues

Song of Moses
Rainbow in Clouds
Wicked Destroyed
No more Sin
Re-Creation

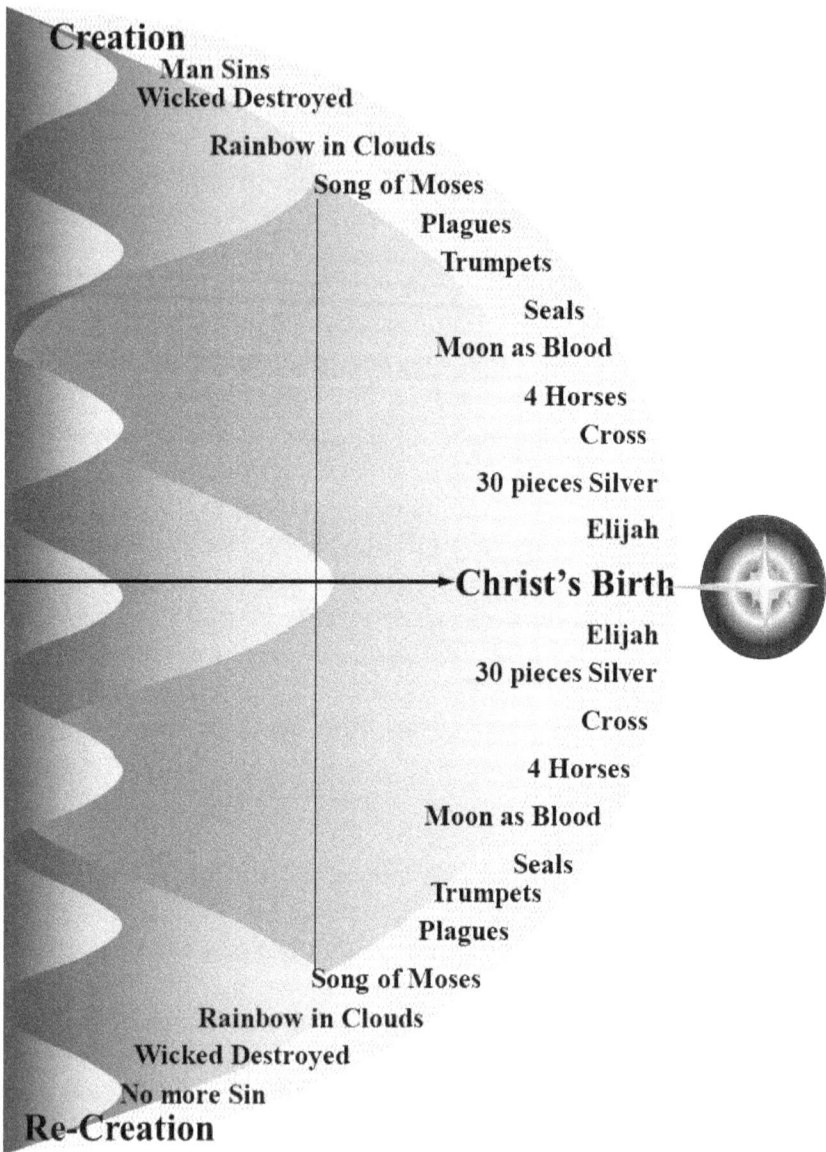

The beginning and ending of the thought, are parallel to one another.[92] The peak of the wave is often the key point. Chiasms provide the rhythm and fabric for the underlying messages. They

---

[92] A well known chiastic structure is found in Genesis 6:10 to 9:19. It can be found in numerous places on the internet under Noah's Ark chiasm.

occur at many wavelengths, frequencies, and amplitudes. The largest of these begins with Creation and ends with Re-Creation. These accounts of mankind's destiny begin in the Garden of Eden, in the Book of Genesis, and continue in the Garden of the New Jerusalem in heaven, as described in the Book of Revelation. The birth of Christ is at the peak of the wave. In this grand wave of the Scriptures, one finds, as in other lessons, that the physical lessons of the Old point to their spiritual fulfillment in the New. For example, physical trumpets of Jericho point to the spiritual trumpets of Revelation. The overall wave form provides many other lessons. The key is that the sins of man triggered the implementation of the Plan of Salvation. Once Jesus made the decision to become man, He committed to a gruesome death on the Cross. It was the ultimate act of LOVE. Another well-known chiastic structure of a shorter wavelength and amplitude is found in the account of Noah.[93]

The main theme of **Noah's Flood chiasm**, is that the world is cleansed of sin and creation is given a new beginning. The cycle of events connect the literal events of the Old with the events of the New. The New Testament refers to the Flood as *the like figure whereunto [even] baptism doth also now save us (not the putting away of the filth of the flesh, but the answer of a good conscience toward God,) by the resurrection of Jesus Christ...[94]* We see the sins of the world, which had accumulated from Adam to Noah, are washed away as a figure (or type), pointing to the washing away of our own sins through the death, burial, and resurrection of Jesus. **Our old life is washed away and is replaced by the new!**

It is written that these Scriptural gems are *the treasures of darkness, and hidden riches of secret places, that thou mayest know that I, the LORD, which call [thee] by thy name, [am] the God of Israel*.[95] What is hidden that will provide the evidence that God exists, that is, that we may know that He is the God of Israel?

---

[93] Genesis 6:9 to 9:19.
[94] 1 Peter 3:20-22.
[95] Isaiah 45:3.

End of Days of Wickedness

A Noah (6:10a)
 B Shem, Ham, and Japheth (10b)
  C Ark (14-16)
   D Flood announced (17)
    E Covenant with Noah (18-20)
     F Food (21)
      G Command to enter the ark (7:1-3)
       H **7 days** (4-5)
        I **7 days** (7-10)
         J Entry to ark (11-15)
          K YHWH shuts Noah in (16)
           L **40 days** (17a)
            M Waters increase (17b-18)
             N Mountains covered (19-20)
              O **150** days water prevail (21-24)
               P God remembered Noah (8:1)
              O' **150** days waters abate (3)
             N' Mountain tops visible (4-5)
            M' Waters abate (5)
           L' **40** days (6a)
          K' Noah opens window of ark (6b)
         J' Raven and dove leave ark (7-9)
        I' 7 days (10-11)
       H' 7 days (12-13)
      G' Command to leave ark (15-17 [22])
     F' Food (9:1-4)
    E' Covenant with all (8-10)
   D' No more world-wide flood (11-17)
  C' Ark (18a)
 B' Shem, Ham and Japheth (18b)
A' Noah (19)

Earth Cleansed of Sin

New Beginning: Rebirth

Chiastic structures are similar to light. The different wavelengths of the chiasms are like the different wavelengths of light refracted by a prism. You might say that the chiasms provide *literary light, or illumination* to be received by our minds in a way similar to how we process color. But something more intriguing than even these chiastic structures is hidden beneath the surface account.

Types, Symbolic Language

Symbolic language is applied like a form of algebra and calculus throughout the Scriptures. In many cases, a symbol is transformed,[96] commonly multiple times. *All these things spake Jesus unto the multitude in parables; and without a parable spake he not unto them: That it might be fulfilled which was spoken by the prophet, saying, I will open my mouth in parables; I will utter things which have been kept secret from the foundation of the world.*[97] In its simplest terms, the embedded code is what is referred to as type and antitype by theologians. Typology has been applied in numerous manuscripts since ancient times. Paul refers to Adam as a type [τύπος] of the one who was to come.[98] Plainly stated, Adam was a type of Christ. In many ways, types are extensions of symbolic language that are given in a prophetic context. Noah's Flood is a figure (or antitypon) of baptism.[99] Even systems like the Old Testament Sanctuary is a type.[100] Likewise, the ceremonies performed within the Sanctuary are patterns and figures. It is written, *the patterns of things in the heavens should be purified with these; but the heavenly things themselves with better sacrifices than these. For Christ is not entered into the holy places made with hands, [which are] the figures of the true; but into heaven itself, now to appear in the presence of God for us...*[101] It is also written, *Christ our passover is sacrificed for us.*[102] Even Old Testament characters such as Adam,[103] Melchizedek,[104] and Isaac[105] are considered types of Christ. Even places are used symbolically. It is written, *which things are an allegory: for these are the two covenants; the one*

---

[96] The transform of the symbol is analogous to a LaPlace transform.
[97] Matthew 13:34, 35.
[98] Romans 5:14; 1 Corinthians 15
[99] 1 Peter 3:21.
[100] Hebrews 9:8, 9.
[101] Hebrews 9:23, 24.
[102] 1 Corinthians 5:7.
[103] Romans 5:14.
[104] Hebrews 5:6, 10.
[105] Hebrews 11:19.

from the mount Sinai, which gendereth to bondage, which is Agar [Hagar]. For this Agar is mount Sinai in Arabia, and answereth to Jerusalem which now is, and is in bondage with her children. But Jerusalem which is above is free, which is the mother of us all.[106]

Objects and actions such as the raising of the serpent in the wilderness are types, for Jesus Himself said, *and as Moses lifted up the serpent in the wilderness, <u>even so must the Son of man be lifted up</u>...*[107] And it is written that *they drank of that spiritual Rock that followed them: and <u>that Rock was Christ.</u>*[108] And in another place, *Jesus said unto them, Verily, verily, I say unto you, Moses gave you not that bread from heaven; but my Father giveth you the true bread from heaven. For the bread of God is he which cometh down from heaven, and giveth life unto the world. Then said they unto him, Lord, evermore give us this bread. And Jesus said unto them, <u>I am the bread of life: he that cometh to me shall never hunger; and he that believeth on me shall never thirst</u>.*[109] But the hidden code transcends chiastic structures, symbolic language, and types. The secret code, hidden since the foundation of the world, is the extension of all of these. And the code is a continuum from the beginning of the Scriptures to the end. How could the 66 books with over 40 distinct authors be connected through a consistent underlying code? Is this an *infallible proof*?[110] I think so. You'll have to decide for yourself.

Ensamples, Event Sequence

Ensamples are a patterns, plays, or templates used as prophetic illustrations of what is coming in the future. In one such instance, the Lord commands that Ezekiel act out the siege of Jerusalem.[111] Ezekiel is required to build a model of Jerusalem from clay and lay

---

[106] Galatians 4:24-26.
[107] John 3:14.
[108] 1 Corinthians 10:4.
[109] John 6:31-35.
[110] Acts 1:3.
[111] Ezekiel chapters 4, 5.

siege to it. He lies on his left side for 390 days (for Israel and Judah), and then only on his right side for forty days. During the 390 days, Ezekiel cuts off hair to represent those that will be lost and eats a starvation diet to symbolize famine. Ezekiel prophesied 40 days against the model of Jerusalem. These mini plays show both the destruction of the city and its temple, and the exile.

Importantly, the **event sequence** of the Old Testament accounts are in the order that the transformed message is found in the future realization. An example is the enactment of the sacrifice of Christ found in the account of Abraham and Isaac. We see that a **series of connections** occur between the events in the account of Isaac in the Old[112] and the account of Jesus in the New:

1. The births of Isaac and Jesus were announced by angels.
2. Their births were claimed to be miracles.
3. They were both beloved sons.
4. They were both sons of Abraham.
5. Both were offered as a sacrifice.
6. Both were to be sacrificed on Mount Moriah (located outside Jerusalem).
7. Both carried the wood for their sacrifice.
8. Both were bound and placed upon the wood.
9. Both were willing to be sacrificed.
10. Both were raised from the altar.
11. Lamb of God, with crown of thorns, the substitute sacrifice.
12. The third day, both are saved from the grip of death.

Helical Transform Function

Ensamples, which are patterns that are used in a given context, like the plays of Ezekiel, point forward to a future set of events. Ezekiel's props and plays prophetically point forward to the fate of Jerusalem and its people. Specifically, he was ordered by God to

---

[112] Genesis 22:1-18.

act out the future events of famine, siege, destruction, and exile. The sequence of events in the plays enacted by Ezekiel projected the future fate of Jerusalem through a connected set of ordered events. This is the basis of event sequence analysis.

One mark of a Divine Author of the Scriptures is continuity of thought and logic connecting the beginning to the end. The wave theory that I addressed as **chiastic waves of literary illumination** can be traced from Genesis to Revelation. In and of themselves, they cannot prove or disprove the existence of a Divine Author. Many think they are just a literary style attributed to human authors. Chiastic wave forms are consistent with a supernatural Author. I don't know how opponents can rationalize that over 40 human authors conspired to continue the wave pattern over a period of more than 1500 years. But there are other wave forms that do require an author that can see the end from the beginning.

I refer to this wave form as a **helical wave transform.** It provides a continuum of logic and connectivity from Genesis to Revelation. The helix can be visualized as a spring, or more appropriately, like a strand of deoxyribose nucleic acid (DNA). The repetition along the Scriptural helix is analogous to the repeated sequence of proteins along a strand of DNA; each one carrying a coded message. In the diagram, you see a visual depiction of a helical waveform. The letters on the helix are **transformed through time** from a symbol represented as "A" that evolves to a future meaning as "**A2**" and to an even more evolved symbol "**A3**" and beyond until they reach their final intended fulfillment. You might say that the initial thought is the seed and the final thought is the fruit. The progression of the transformation of thought is often from a literal or natural thought to a "spiritual" or supernatural thought. As you can see in the figure, the three dimensional helix can be projected to a two dimensional surface as a circle. A through H represent a sequence of events that are repeated as a transformed set of thoughts or events: A2 to H2.

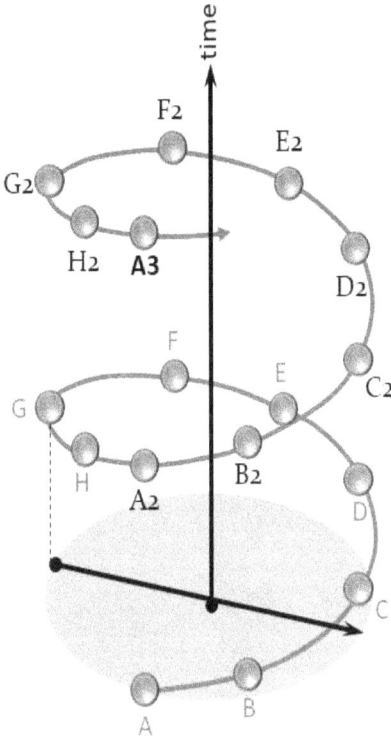

Helical Wave Transform Projected on a Plane. Variable A is a shadow of Variable A2 which in turn is a shadow of **A3**.

A is transformed to A2 and then to A3 as a function of time.

$$A \longrightarrow A2 \longrightarrow A3$$

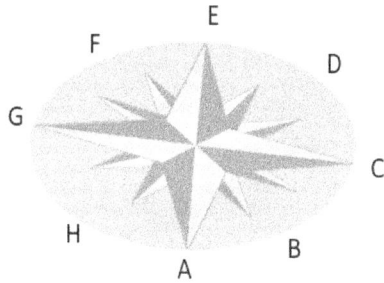

The author uses the helical waveform to take your mind from the world you are familiar with, to a world you have never seen before. It is an amazing communication and teaching device by the School Master. As an example, we consider the sequence of events from Chapter 1 to Chapter 9 of the Book of Genesis. Creation sets time in motion for mankind. In the context of the Creation of Genesis, we see the beginning as the first year, the first month, and the first day, or **111**. In our example, we next come to the Fall of Man. Man is then ushered into the wilderness outside the Garden to till the ground. We next see the introduction of a sacrificial system through the account of Abel. It is written, Abel **brought of the firstlings of the flock**…and **the Lord had respect of Abel and his offering**. But out of jealousy Cain slew his brother and **sin lieth at the door**. What door? The Sanctuary door, as we'll see later.

The Door to the Ark will soon be Closed

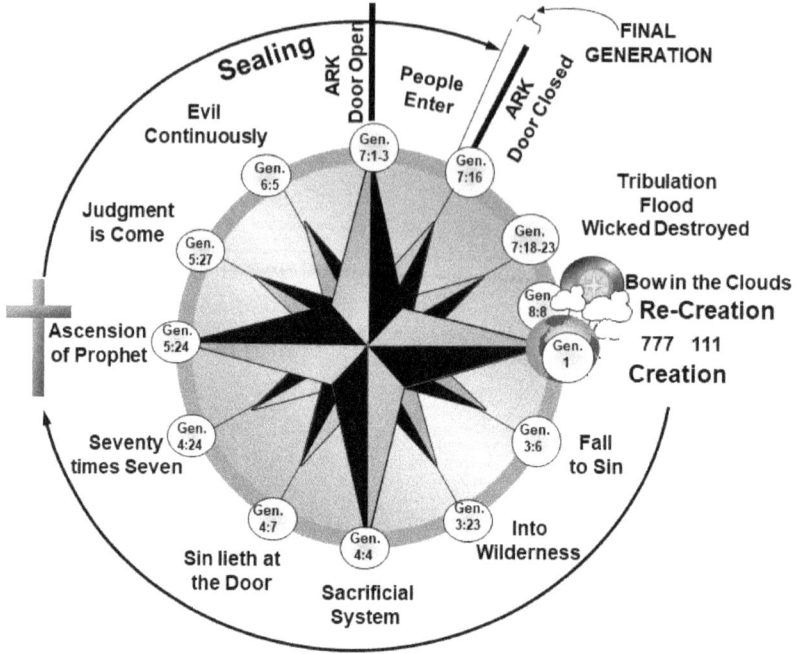

Next we hear about the phrase seventy times seven which echoes the words of Christ. ***Then came Peter to him, and said, Lord, how oft shall my brother sin against me, and I forgive him? till seven times? Jesus saith unto him, I say not unto thee, Until seven times: but, Until seventy times seven.***[113] Then we hear of the Ascension which foreshadows the ascension of Jesus. This is followed by judgment and a time when evil will be continuous; even to a time of trouble such as never was. We then hear of the sealing and the Ark of Noah which connects our thought to the sealing of those that have given their lives to Christ before the Ark in the Holiest Place in heaven![114] We learn of the open door to the Ark that the people may enter in. But once the door to Noah's ark is closed just as the door to the Ark in heaven is closed, there is no more opportunity for redemption. Once the door to the two arks are closed there is tribulation and the wicked are destroyed. And at

---

[113] Matthew 18:21, 22.
[114] Hebrews 8:1, 2.

the end of the tribulation there is the appearance of the rainbow in the clouds pointing to the Second Coming of Jesus. And with the Second Coming, there is a Re-Creation and a new beginning. After the dove is sent three times after 7 days each[115] (**777**) we see in Genesis 8:13 that the new beginning is given as the first year, in the first month, in the first day of the month (**111**) and a new Creation is established. We see that we have come full circle from Creation to Re-Creation! We see that the sequence of events from the days of Creation to the end of Noah's Flood point to the sequence of events that will occur in the end of time. Jesus said, *as it was in the days of Noe, so shall it be also in the days of the Son of man. They did eat, they drank, they married wives, they were given in marriage, until the day that Noe entered into the ark, and the flood came, and destroyed them all.*[116] Much may be gleaned from this cycle of creation, sacrifice, judgment, sealing, the closed door to the ark, tribulation, and the rainbow signifying the Second Coming; even beginning with a **111** and ending with a **777** and restarting with a **111**…!!! Perhaps you are aware of at least one other cycle between the account of Noah and the account of Christ and the end times! I suggest you explore the account of Moses and the Exodus where the Ark of the Covenant first appears in the Scriptures. We are just beginning to acquire the methods to unearth *the treasures of darkness, and hidden riches of secret places, that thou mayest know that I, the LORD, which call [thee] by thy name, [am] the God of Israel.*[117] The treasures that we will unearth provide a foundation of Faith based upon the evidence that is provided within the Scriptures. **From this evidence, we are told that we will know that the Author of the Scriptures is the God of Israel!**

Helical Transform Waves

A student of the Scriptures can readily see three cycles that originate from passages of Creation to Noah's Flood. Another

---

[115] Genesis 8:8-12.
[116] Luke 17:26, 27.
[117] Isaiah 45:3.

such set of helical waves connect the Scriptures from Genesis to Revelation. I refer to these as the Promised Land Wave Form.

The typical cycle begins in Chapter 12 of Genesis. In the account, Abram is promised (a) that out of His seed[118] will come a great nation. Next there is a famine (b) in the land.[119] The woman (c), Sarai, is desired. The woman was taken into captivity (d) by Pharaoh. The Pharaoh is plagued (e) by the Lord. The woman is released (f). The woman is given wealth (g). This helical transform can be traced at least 7 times from Genesis to Revelation:

1 Abram and Sarai (Genesis 12)

2 Abraham and Sarah (Genesis 20)

3 Isaac and Rebekah (Genesis 26)

4 Moses/Joshua and the woman → Israel (Exodus/Joshua)

5 Israel and Cyrus (New earthly Jerusalem) (Isaiah/Daniel)

6 Israel and Jesus (heavenly Jerusalem) (Gospels/Revelation)

7 Bride and Bridegroom (Christ and the Church) (Revelation)

I provide you with the 7 cycles for your consideration and study. What you will see, is that the key events (a through g) are transformed through the 7 cycles as a method of teaching; and as a means of connecting the earthly with the heavenly. The person Sarai/Sarah/Rebekah begins as a single woman. The woman is transformed into the nation Israel. The nation of Israel connects to the earthly Jerusalem which points to the heavenly Jerusalem which is the Church, and finally the Bride of Christ! Follow the transformation of the other parameters, especially the famine, captivity, the plagues, and the release of the woman.

---

[118] Genesis 12:7.
[119] Genesis 12:10.

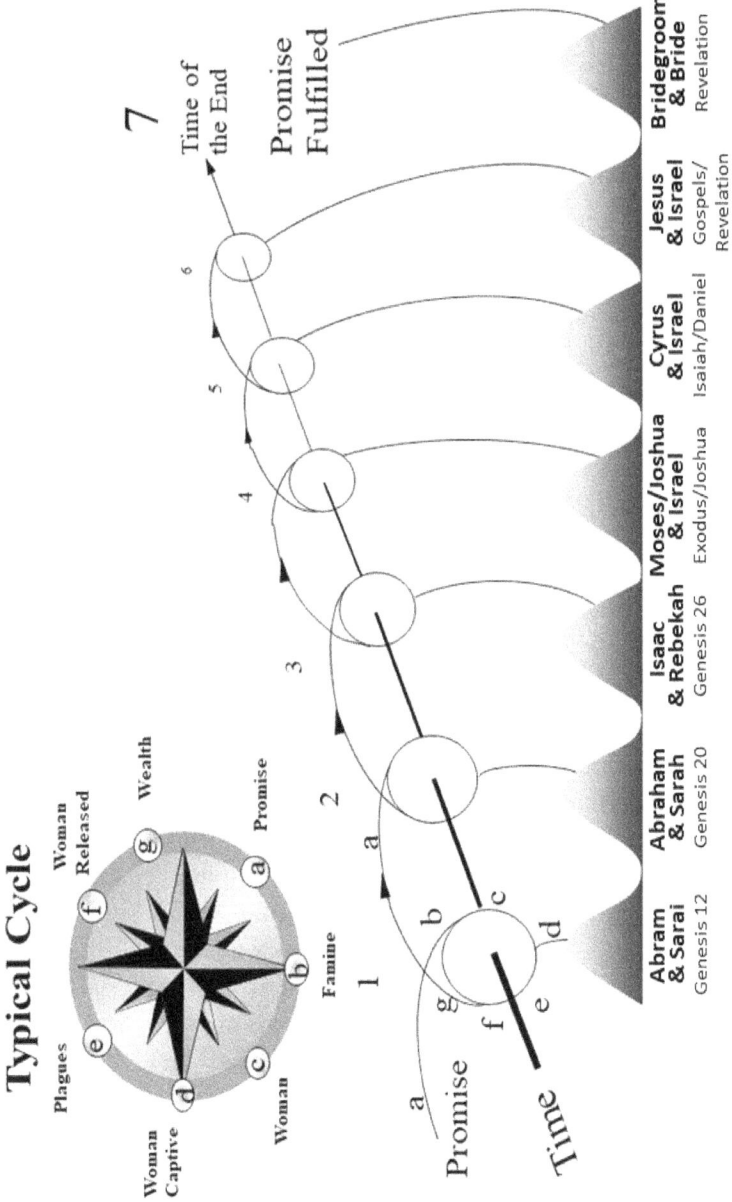

Promised Land Wave Form

Typical Cycle

Woman Released

Wealth

Plagues

g

f

a Promise

e

b

Woman Captive

d

c

Woman

Famine

1

2

3

4

5

6

7

Time of the End

Promise Fulfilled

Promise

Time

Abram & Sarai	Abraham & Sarah	Isaac & Rebekah	Moses/Joshua & Israel	Cyrus & Israel	Jesus & Israel	Bridegroom & Bride
Genesis 12	Genesis 20	Genesis 26	Exodus/Joshua	Isaiah/Daniel	Gospels/Revelation	Revelation

Scriptural DNA: B-DNA, Z-DNA

The Scriptures exhibit both right-handed and left-handed helical wave transforms. As a way of background, the normal form of DNA, as first described by Watson and Crick,[120] is predominately a right-handed helix and is referred to as B-DNA. This is determined by the overall stability of the stacking interactions, which favor right-handed helices. There are rare forms of DNA, such as Z-DNA that are left-handed. This left-handed DNA is rich in GC proteins. GC stands for its guanine-cytosine content which make up a percentage of nitrogenous bases on a DNA. Likewise, the Scriptures exhibit a right-handed (clockwise) helical wave transform pattern (like B-DNA). The right-handed helical wave transform structure is illustrated above as the Creation to Noah cycle and the Promised Land Wave Form. But there is also a left-handed (counterclockwise) DNA pattern (like Z-DNA) that is found in the Sanctuary and the travels of Israel discussed later!

Golden Key: 52 Factorial

So what could be even more compelling? Certainly, the helical waveform that deliberately transforms earthly symbols to the realm of the supernatural is compelling and verifiable. Yet, the greatest evidence is soon to be unfolded. The evidence is hidden behind the surface account of the Scriptures in plain sight. It is by far more compelling than the chiastic waves of literary light that connect the Old and New Testament accounts. It is far more compelling than the helical transforms that connect Genesis with Revelation. How could either of these have been constructed without the guidance of a Being outside the framework of time? In my mind, both of these are consistent with the existence of God.

---

[120] Watson, J.D. and F.H.C. Crick, Molecular Structure of Nucleic Acids, A Structure for Deoxyribose Nucleic Acid. April 25, 1953, pp. 737-738. Nature Publishing Group.

Yet when these lines of evidence are taken together, with event sequence analysis, I am left without doubt. God exists!

In the case of Isaac, we saw 12 simple connections in the life of Isaac that connected him to events surrounding the First Coming of Christ, **in the same order**. We could assign probabilities to approximate the likeliness of this occurrence. But in sharing this with another scientist, that I'll refer to as Dr. Greg, he proposed that I apply factorial analysis. Since the 2 characters (Isaac and Jesus) have 12 common connections in the same order, this correlation can be crudely approximated as 12 factorial which is 4.8 times 10 to the eighth power or 4.8×10^8. This is far more unlikely than death by an insect bite. In the following chapters, I reveal Old Testament characters that have 52 or more connections in the same order with the sequence of events in the account of Christ, within the framework of the Plan of Salvation. I choose 52 events since the reader can readily find comparisons and implications of 52 factorial in the realm of card playing statistics.[121] Simply put, the probability of 52 events occurring independently, in the same order, is like finding a single atom in the Milky Way galaxy (8.0×10^{67}) by chance.

The Golden Key is the event sequence given in the New Testament from the War in Heaven, to the Fall of Man, to the events in the life of Christ from His birth to His Ascension, to the events in the Heavenly Courts including the Judgment, to the Seals, to the Trumpets, to the Second Coming, and to the reconciliation of man with God in the New Jerusalem. The event sequence is used as a key in searching the Old Testament, just as gene sequencing is used!

---

[121] https://ed.ted.com/lessons/how-many-ways-can-you-arrange-a-deck-of-cards-yannay-khaikin

CRACKING GOD'S SECRET CODE

And we have seen and do testify that the Father sent the Son [to be] the Saviour of the world.[122] *Wherefore seeing we also are compassed about with so GREAT A CLOUD OF WITNESSES, let us lay aside every weight, and the sin which doth so easily beset [us], and let us run with patience the race that is set before us*[123]

A golden key is required to open God's Secret Code. We find that events in the lives of Old Testament characters parallel events in the life of Christ. These events are often symbolically tied. *These [are] the words which I spake unto you, while I was yet with you, that <u>all things must be fulfilled, which were written in the law of Moses, and [in] the prophets, and [in] the psalms, concerning me</u>. Then <u>opened he their understanding</u>, that they might understand the scriptures...*[124] Christ declared in numerous places that the characters of the Old Testament are either cast as types or shadows of Himself. Thus, we proceed by cross-examining events in the parallel lives of the Great Cloud of Witnesses. But could there be upwards of 52 parallel events and more?

---

[122] 1 John 4:14.
[123] Hebrews 12:1
[124] Luke 24:44, 45

4   1st Witness: Joseph, Savior of the World

O Shepherd of Israel, thou that leadest Joseph like a flock; thou that dwellest [between] the cherubims, shine forth.[125] *... O God, ... cause thy face to shine; and we shall be saved.* <u>*This he ordained in Joseph [for] a testimony, when he went out through the land of Egypt: [where] I heard a language [that] I understood not.*</u> [126]

By the year 2000, I began an extensive study of the Scriptures. At that time, God's existence still remained a mystery to me. One evening I found myself wanting to believe that God existed, but the evidence was incomplete. Even though there were hundreds of prophecies that were <u>apparently</u> fulfilled by events in the life of Christ, I felt that the jury was still out. You might say that there remained a veil of unbelief, perhaps a learned bias, over my mind that kept me from seeing the deeper evidence within the Scriptures. I had come across a passage in Paul's writings that spoke directly to me. The passage said, ***But their minds were blinded: for until this day remaineth the same veil untaken away in the reading of the old testament; which [veil] is done away in Christ. But even unto this day, when***

---

[125] Psalm 80:1, 2.
[126] Psalm 81:5.

Moses is read, the veil is upon their heart. Nevertheless <u>when it</u> <u>[the heart] shall turn to the Lord, the veil shall be taken away.</u> Now the Lord is that Spirit: and where the Spirit of the Lord [is], there [is] liberty.[127]

Emmaus Experience

I clearly remember sitting in my home office one day, early in the years of my quest to disprove the Bible and the existence of God. I sat with the Bible on my lap after hours of study. In that special moment, I prayed earnestly saying, God, if you really do exist, please provide me the evidence. If I can't find the necessary evidence, I will do everything that I can to disprove your existence. In the instant that followed, I had a most amazing experience. It was as if the veil that was upon my heart and mind was suddenly taken away. **When I looked upon the passages in Genesis 37, I saw Jesus in the account of Joseph in a very clear way.** It was my Emmaus experience. For the Scriptures say that Jesus showed His followers passages in the writings of Moses, the psalms, and the prophets, that testified of Himself. ***Then <u>opened he their</u>*** ***<u>understanding</u>, that they might understand the scriptures.***[128] Likewise, Jesus opened the veil of understanding for me.

Golden Key to the Code

Joseph, the Son of Jacob, the Ancient of Days, stood before me in the text just as if I were reading the timeline in the account of Jesus in the writings of Matthew, Mark, Luke, John, Paul, and the other apostles, especially the Revelation of John. I was most amazed because the account wasn't in a haphazard order. Rather, **the account of the events in the life of Joseph were in <u>parallel order</u> with the events in the life of Jesus more than a thousand years in advance. The golden key to cracking the encryption in the Old Testament is the pattern and sequence of events given in**

---

[127] 2 Corinthians 3:14-17.
[128] Luke 24:45.

the New Testament. And central to that Plan, are the events of the birth, ministry, death, burial, and resurrection of Jesus. But it doesn't stop there. The author of the book of Genesis must have deemed the account of Joseph to be exceedingly important, because he devotes 14 chapters to him. The account is far lengthier than any other account in the Book of Genesis. It is far lengthier than the account in the Garden of Eden; it is far lengthier than the account of Noah and the Flood; it is far lengthier than the account of Abraham. Why? **I have since concluded that the Author places His greatest emphasis on the account of Joseph because it uniquely provides the panoramic view of the Plan of Salvation.** Amazingly, Joseph's account begins with the hate borne of egotism and jealousy in the heavenly Canaan where Israel, the ancient of days resided, and ends with the re-uniting of the ancient of days and Israel's people; just as the account of Jesus begins with the controversy in heaven and ends with the reuniting of God, the Ancient of Days, and His people of Spiritual Israel.

Joseph, Shadow of Jesus

Joseph's life events quickly began to unfold before me, beginning in parallel with events that are documented in the Plan of Salvation. Joseph, like Jesus, is of the ⬚[1][129] **lineage of Father Abraham.** He was the very Abraham that talked with the Lord; the very Abraham that was given the Promise.[130] He is the same Abraham that the Lord directed to take Joseph's ⬚[2] **grandfather Isaac** to the Mountain to be slain as a lamb. In that account of Joseph's ancestors, Father Abraham asked, *Wherewith shall I come before the Lord, and bow myself before the high God? Shall I come before Him with burnt offerings, with calves of a year old? Will the Lord be pleased with thousands of rams, or with ten thousands of rivers of oil?* <u>*shall I give my first-born for*</u>

---

[129] Numbers in squares represent points in common between the character and Jesus. Only selected points are provided. Numerous additional in depth comparisons are provided in subsequent volumes.
[130] Genesis 12:7

my transgression, the fruit of my body for the sin of my soul?[131]
Abraham's question was a deliberate rhetorical question. For
**Isaac would represent Jesus, the First Born, as the lamb to be
slain for the sin of our souls.**

And Isaac spoke unto Abraham his father, and said, *My father:
and he said, Here [am] I, my son. And he said, Behold the fire
and the wood: but where [is] the lamb for a burnt offering? And
Abraham said, My son, God will provide himself a lamb for a
burnt offering: so they went both of them together.*[132] For it was
*by faith Abraham, when he was tried, offered up Isaac: and he
that had received the promises offered up his only begotten [son].
Of whom it was said, That in Isaac shall thy seed be called:
Accounting that God [was] able to raise [him] up, even from the
dead; from whence also he received him in a figure.*[133]

And through their faithfulness in following the commands of the
Lord God, Father Abraham was given a vision of the resurrection
of the Messiah. It is written, *Abraham rejoiced to see my day and
he saw it and was glad.*[134] And having seen the resurrected Jesus
in the vision, Father Abraham went ahead with the sacrifice of
Isaac, his son, his only son. Why? Because Father Abraham was
convinced that the Promise of the Seed must pass through Joseph's
grandfather Isaac. Father Abraham was so confident that if Isaac
should die as a sacrifice, he was convinced that Isaac would be
resurrected just as Jesus, the Savior of the World, would be
resurrected. For their faithfulness, the Angel of the Lord stopped
the execution of Isaac and provided a **Lamb with a crown of
thorns as the substitute**.[135]

Like Isaac, Joseph's life was a deliberate foreshadow of the Plan of
Salvation. It was an ensample for those in the Last Days when
Jesus shall bring His people into the Promised Land. Joseph is
known as the 3 **son of Israel,** 4 **the Ancient of Days**. His home is

---

[131] Micah 6:6, 7.
[132] Genesis 22:7, 8.
[133] Hebrews 11:17-19.
[134] John 8:56; Galatians 3:6-18.
[135] Genesis 22:2-18.

in the ⑤ **land of Canaan, the Promised Land** of his forefathers. Joseph's name means ⑥ **"Savior of the World;"** all points directly connecting him with Jesus, the true Savior of the World.

Joseph's ⑦ **brothers were jealous** of the love that the Father, the Ancient of Days, shed upon Joseph, just as Satan is jealous of the love that the Father shed upon Jesus. And it was then that Joseph took the ⑧ **evil report** [136]of the rebellion of his brothers to his Father Israel, just as Jesus took the evil report of Satan's rebellion to God the Father, the Ancient of Days. Joseph's Father Israel so loved him that he was set aside from his brethren, signifying this by clothing him in a ⑨ **coat of many colors**[137] just like the very **rainbow coat of light**[138] that covers Jesus on the heavenly throne. ⑩ **Joseph could see the future** and he revealed that ⑪ **he would reign and have dominion over his brothers** and that ⑫ **everyone would bow down before him and obey him.**[139] Joseph's ⑬ **prophetic view of the future was a foreshadowing of the omniscience of Jesus**. And Joseph's prophecy looked ahead to the far distant future when *every knee would bow,* just as Jesus saw His Second Coming when *every knee shall bow, every tongue shall swear*[140] to Him that He is Lord.

As I listened, my mind was stirred and awakened as the account of Joseph revealed to me one event after another that connected him to Jesus. He is the son of Israel, the Ancient of Days who lived in the Promised Land. His name means "Savior of the World." He wears the **Coat of Many Colors** like **the rainbow robe of light that covers Jesus**. His brothers were jealous of him and rebelled like the rebellion of Satan and his angels. And in the end, every knee would bow to both of them. I was intrigued and I wondered how the Author of the account knew of Jesus more than a thousand years in advance. How did this Author know of Jesus in such **ordered detail,** so far in advance?

---

[136] Genesis 37:2.
[137] Genesis 37:3.
[138] Revelation 4:3.
[139] Genesis 37:5-10.
[140] Isaiah 45:23; Romans 14:11; Philippians 2:10.

The Commission

Israel's 14 **sheep were being taken care for by the very brethren that hated him**. Israel, the Ancient of Days gave the son 15 the **commission to go into the world** to find 16 the **Lost Sheep of Israel**. Israel said, *Go, I pray thee, see whether it be well with thy brethren, and well with the flocks and bring me word again.*[141] So without hesitation Joseph, like Jesus, responded, 17 *Here [am I].* And even before Joseph left the realm of Canaan, he could hear the yet to be spoken words of the Ancient of Days saying, 18 *Forgive, I pray thee now, the trespass of thy brethren, and their sin; for they did unto thee evil: and now, … forgive the trespass of the servants of the God of thy father.*[142] Joseph, like Jesus, knew beforehand that 19 **his Father** *sent him to save their lives by a great deliverance.*[143] Joseph was sent to fulfill the vision that would point to the coming of the resurrected Jesus.

At the Father's request, Joseph left the comforts of Canaan and headed to find the Father's sheep. Joseph 20 **crossed through** *the vale*, **a chasm that separates Canaan from the world**, to begin his mission. When Joseph entered into the world he was found 21 *wandering in the field*[144] by a certain man. And this 22 **voice in the wilderness**[145] pointed the way to the lost flock of Israel. As I read the text, I realized that the voice in the wilderness was referring to none other than John the Baptist because I recalled the words of Matthew: *For this is he that was spoken of by the prophet Esaias, saying, The voice of one crying in the wilderness, Prepare ye the way of the Lord, make his paths straight.*[146]

As I grasped the testimony of Joseph, my mind was stirred. It was as if I had heard all of this before. The events in the life of Joseph

---

[141] Genesis 37:13, 14.
[142] Genesis 50:17.
[143] Genesis 45:7.
[144] Genesis 37:15. Hebrew word "sadeh" meaning areas occupied by men.
[145] Matthew 3:3.
[146] Matthew 3:3.

were pointing to the events in the life of Jesus more than 1700 years into the future! How could the Author of this Guardian's account have known about the life of Jesus in such detail? After all, the events in the Guardian's life were a matter of recorded history more than a thousand years before the events were to unfold in the life of Jesus. **Could it really have been God?**

Plot to Kill Him

It was then that I understood the words spoken of in the new testament that say, *Even as <u>Abraham believed God</u>... it was accounted to him for righteousness. Know ye therefore that they which are of faith, the same are the children of Abraham. And the scripture, foreseeing that God would justify the heathen through faith, <u>preached before the gospel unto Abraham</u>, [saying], In thee shall all nations be blessed. So then they which be of faith are blessed with faithful Abraham... Christ hath redeemed us from the curse of the law, being made a curse for us: for it is written, Cursed [is] every one that hangeth on a tree: That the blessing of Abraham might come on the Gentiles through Jesus Christ; that we might receive the promise of the Spirit through faith.*[147]

With my refreshed understanding of the Scriptures, I could almost anticipate what events would occur next. Sure enough, the text said that Joseph's |23| **brethren were already conspiring to slay him**[148] just as they conspired to kill Jesus from the beginning. They were |24| **jealous and threatened by the visions of Joseph and Jesus**. |25| **They could not imagine themselves bowing down** to Joseph or Jesus as if either were a King.

As I continued to read the testimony of Joseph, my mind recalled how they conspired to kill Jesus. I remembered that there was the day that Jesus stepped forward to speak in the synagogue to announce His Messiahship saying, *The Spirit of the Lord [is]*

---

[147] Galatians 3:6-14.
[148] Genesis 37:18.

upon me, because he hath anointed me to preach the gospel to the poor; he hath sent me to heal the brokenhearted, to preach deliverance to the captives, and recovering of sight to the blind, to set at liberty them that are bruised... And he began to say unto them, This day is this scripture fulfilled in your ears...when they heard these things, [they] were filled with wrath, and rose up, and ...<u>led him unto the brow of the hill whereon their city was built, that they might cast him down headlong</u>. [149] *And later he angered them saying, Your father Abraham rejoiced to see my day: and he saw [it], and was glad. ... Jesus said unto them, Verily, verily, I say unto you, Before Abraham was, I am.* <u>Then took they up stones to cast at him...</u>[150]

And as I continued to read about the account of Joseph, I could almost hear him say, 26 **they stripped me of my robe**[151] and 27 **cast me**[152] into 28 **the tomb.** And afterwards they came 29 **bearing spicery and balm and myrrh.**[153] And it was his brother 30 **Judah that sold him** *for twenty* 31 **pieces of silver,**[154] the price of a slave. 32 Judah **sold his identity**[155] and his soul 33 **in exchange for the lamb.** And when 34 **he went to make the transaction to retrieve his identity, he couldn't get it back**.[156]

I was amazed at the detail with which the text spoke of Jesus through the account of Joseph. I recalled how they *cast lots*[157] at the foot of the Cross for His precious blood-stained robe, and how they laid him in the tomb and the women would later come bearing *spices, balm and myrrh*.[158] And wasn't it Judas, named in the account of Joseph, that sold his soul [identity][159] and desperately

---

149 Luke 4:18, 21, 28-30.
150 John 8:56-59.
151 Genesis 37:23.
152 Genesis 37:24.
153 Genesis 37:25.
154 Genesis 37:26-28.
155 Genesis 38:18.
156 Genesis 38:20.
157 Matthew 27:35; John 19:24.
158 Mark 16:1; John 19:39.
159 Genesis 38:18.

tried to return the 30 *pieces of silver* to the Pharisees but they would not accept it?[160] And wasn't it Jesus, like Joseph, that was falsely accused?

Ascension

As the text of the account of Joseph continued, I could hardly believe what I was hearing. Was he speaking about himself or of Jesus? The foreknowledge of events surrounding the details of the death, burial, and resurrection of Jesus continued to my amazement. <u>**The scientist in me knew that the order of events could not be by coincidence**</u>. The life record was a revelation of Jesus and His Plan of Salvation. It was an incredibly ingenious way of hiding the secret code, hidden from the foundation of the world. The plaintext hid the cyphertext in plain sight.

Joseph, like Jesus, was |35| **falsely accused** and |36| **sentenced with two criminals**; |37| **one was saved** and |38| **one was lost**. Joseph like Jesus, let them know that |39| **after three days** one would be raised.[161] When Joseph like Jesus |40| **ascended to the Palace** they were given |41| **change of Kingly garments**[162] and both were given the title |42| **"Savior"** and |43| **"Revealer of Secrets."**[163] And because of their revelations |44| **both were seated upon the throne** as |45| **second in all of the Kingdom**. And when |46| **their brethren were brought before them,** |47| **they bowed down before Joseph and Jesus** with their faces to the ground in fulfillment of the prophecy.[164] |48| **Both tested them** and |49| **both listened to the confessions of their hearts** and then |50| **they revealed themselves to them.**[165]

---

[160] Matthew 27:3-6.
[161] Genesis 40:12-19.
[162] Genesis 41:14.
[163] Genesis 41:45; Daniel 2:47.
[164] Genesis 42:6.
[165] Genesis 45:1.

And again, to my amazement, the Guardian continued to reveal what had transpired at the Cross and beyond. One of the criminals with Jesus was given the Promise of eternal life just as was recorded in the account of Joseph. Likewise Jesus, after His death and burial was resurrected, and exchanged his grave clothes for a royal change of garments. Joseph appeared secretly to them just as Jesus had appeared secretly to the two on the Road to Emmaus.

For the next several hours, the underlying text of the account of Joseph continued to reveal events surrounding the life and mission of Jesus, the one we know as Savior of the World. But most of all, as a scientist, I wondered how nearly 100 events in the life of Joseph could be in the same order as they unfolded in the life and mission of Jesus, more than a thousand years in advance. The encrypted events of the life of Jesus were cleverly hidden behind the account of Joseph. **The encryption was deliberate. WHY?**

Great Deliverance

And Joseph, the *Savior of the World*, said, 51 **Now therefore be not grieved, nor angry with yourselves, that ye sold me hither: for God did send me before you to preserve life...** 52 **God sent me before you to preserve you a posterity in the earth, and to save your lives by a great deliverance.**[166] And again I heard him say, 53 **To all of them he gave each man changes of raiment.**[167] Likewise, Jesus will give the redeemed *white robes*[168] of righteousness. And did not God say, 54 **I will go down with thee into Egypt; and** 55 **I will also surely bring thee up [again].**[169] 56 **The sceptre shall not depart from Judah, nor a lawgiver from between his feet, until Shiloh come; and** 57 **unto Him shall the gathering of the people [be].**[170] And at that time

---

[166] Genesis 45:5, 7.
[167] Genesis 45:22.
[168] Revelation 7:13, 14.
[169] Genesis 46:4.
[170] Genesis 49:10.

went up 58 **chariots and** 59 **a very great company**[171] as 60 **the clouds of heaven and** 61 **Joseph, like Jesus, went up with the people to meet Father Israel.** And there were many more hidden events that will be revealed in a more detailed book on the account of Joseph.

I was certain that this Guardian of the Secret Code was speaking of the resurrection yet to come. And I recalled reading that, *behold, [one] like the Son of man came with the clouds of heaven, and came to the Ancient of days, and they brought him near before him. And there was given him dominion, and glory, and a kingdom, that all people, nations, and languages, should serve him: his dominion [is] an everlasting dominion, which shall not pass away, and his kingdom [that] which shall not be destroyed.*[172]

And at the end of the Guardian's written testimony I could hear Jesus saying, *Tell ye, and bring [them] near; yea, let them take counsel together: who hath declared this from ancient time? [who] hath told it from that time? [have] not I the LORD? and [there is] no God else beside me; a just God and a Saviour; [there is] none beside me. Look unto me, and be ye saved, all the ends of the earth: for I [am] God, and [there is] none else. I have sworn by myself, the word is gone out of my mouth [in] righteousness, and shall not return, That unto me every knee shall bow, every tongue shall swear. Surely, shall [one] say, in the LORD have I righteousness and strength: [even] to him shall [men] come; and all that are incensed against [me] shall be ashamed...in the LORD shall all the seed of Israel be justified, and shall glory.*[173]

---

[171] Genesis 50:9. See Psalm 68:17 God's chariots are angels.
[172] Daniel 7:13, 14.
[173] Isaiah 45:21-25.

Testimony of Joseph

He's the Son of Israel, the Ancient of Days
Known as the Savior of the World in the heavenly
Canaan; He learns of the EVIL REPORT
His Father gives him a rainbow Coat of Many Colors
He will reign and have dominion over all
He accepts his father's commission and crosses the
chasm that separates Canaan from the world

The VOICE OF ONE IN THE WILDERNESS directs
him to the Lost Sheep of Israel
The brethren plot to kill him
They strip him of his robe and cast him in the pit
They come bearing spices, balm and myrrh
Judah sold him out for silver; Judah sold his identity
(soul) in exchange for the Lamb
He is falsely accused
Two were with him; one was saved, one was lost
THREE DAYS

He ascended and was Seated upon the throne as
Second in Command of the Kingdom
They bowed down to him, faces to the ground
He revealed himself to them
God sent him ahead of them to save lives by a
GREAT DELIVERANCE

He gave them change of raiment
Unto him shall the gathering of the people be
They went up in chariots to their new home

Divinely Intertwined Lives (52!)

As I listened to Joseph's testimony, I identified nearly 100 points that connect the events in his life to those of Jesus in the same order.[174] I would soon learn that events in the lives of numerous other Guardians also connect and intertwine with the account of Jesus, like strands of DNA. How could the accounts of characters like Joseph, Isaac, Samson, David, Elisha, Jonah, Moses, Joshua, and many others be deliberately choreographed hundreds of years in advance? Jesus claims that the Old Testament is all about Him. What if His claim is true? Theologians refer to this as typology. Certainly the Guardian is a type of Christ but he is far, far, more than a type; **it is the PROOF OF THE EXISTENCE OF GOD**.

Scientists approach this kind of correlation as an **event sequence analysis**. Even the probability of 52 events occurring in order (like selecting the same card out of each of two decks of cards in the same order over and over again) is analyzed by factorial analysis. 52 factorial ($52! = 8 \times 10^{67}$) is the probability of finding a single atom in the Milky Way galaxy! 70 factorial ($70! = 1 \times 10^{100}$) is like finding a single atom in the entire universe! And the sequence in the account of Joseph alone, exceeds 70 factorial!

THE ENCRYPTED SEQUENCE OF EVENTS HAS TO BE DELIBERATE! A SUPERNATURAL BEING IS SENDING MANKIND A MESSAGE. BUT WHO? WHAT? AND WHY?

COULD GOD EXIST?

WHAT OTHER EXPLANATION IS THERE?

---

[174] Alexander, D.H. 2018. Joseph, Savior of the World, Guardian of the Code.

5 2nd *Witness: Samson, Power of God*

And the angel of the LORD appeared unto the woman, and said unto her, Behold now, thou [art] barren, and bearest not: but thou shalt conceive, and bear a son... and he shall begin to deliver Israel ...Then the woman came and told her husband, saying, A man of God came unto me, and his countenance [was] like the countenance of an angel of God, very terrible: ...But he said unto me, Behold, thou shalt conceive, and bear a son; ...for the child shall be a Nazarite to God from the womb to the day of his death.[175]

The author of Samson's account in the Book of Judges provides a dramatic contrast between Samson and Christ, as if the two, in their literal accounts, are polar opposites. Yet in my opinion, the account of Samson is the best example of Christ in the Old Testament, through the hidden cyphertext, of course. In the literal accounts, Jesus kept His vows whereas Samson soon broke his sacred vows of a Nazarite. Samson was easily infatuated by the charms of lewd women. Samson was the very one that lost all sense of his sacred duty and honor. He was the one that broke the pledge laid upon his parents by the Secret Angel. And he killed thousands. And

---

[175] Judges 13:3-7 .

that makes Samson's hidden encryption of the life and ministry of Jesus all the more incredibly amazing and engaging. I have presented the following analysis to more individuals than I can count from college professors, colleagues, Pastors, adults, and young children. All have been excited and amazed by the unlocked encryption and its hidden message. And there is no doubt in my mind that the hidden encryption testifies of Jesus in significant detail, hundreds of years before the birth of Christ. And the events in the account of Samson connect to at least 52 points in the life of Christ in parallel! I provide selected connections between Samson and Jesus below and a separate volume to follow.

Birth of the Deliverer

[1] **Samson, like Jesus, was borne when Israel was oppressed and in bondage.**[176] Israel had been in captivity for forty years[177] when the announcement of Samson's birth came. [2] **The angel of the LORD appeared unto Samson's mother, *and said unto her, Behold now, thou [art] barren, and bearest not: but thou shalt conceive, and bear a son.*[178]** [3] Samson's birth **was a miracle birth** because his mother was ***barren and bare not.***[179] She was convinced that she would remain barren for all of her days. Likewise, an angel visited Christ's mother, Mary, and announced her miracle birth. The mothers of Samson and Jesus were told that they would bear a [4] **Holy child**; a [5] **Nazarite unto God from the womb**[180] dedicated to be the [6] **Deliverer**[181] of Israel. After both of their [7] **mothers were visited by the Angel of the Lord** [8] **both of their father's were visited by an Angel of the Lord.** [182] Both were told by the Angels of their miracle births. The Angels first visited their mothers and then they visited their fathers. Manoah, a Danite, and his wife were given strict instructions not to

---

[176] Judges 13:1.
[177] Judges 13:1.
[178] Judges 13:3.
[179] Judges 13:2.
[180] Judges 13:4-7.
[181] Judges 13:5.
[182] Judges 13:8-14.

cut Samson's hair nor allow his mother to drink strong drink or eat unclean foods for Samson was to be raised Holy and [9] **set apart for the mission that God had in store for him.** Likewise, Jesus was Holy and set apart. Manoah inquired of the name of the Angel and the Angel replied saying, *Why askest thou thus after my name, seeing it [is] secret?*[183] The Angel of the Lord is the *Secret, I AM*,[184] the very Jesus that kept His name secret from the foundation of the world so that His Plan to Rescue mankind would be successful. Samson was named after the Secret Angel that had performed miracles for his parents. They named him Samson, which means [10] **Like the Sun,** since Jesus is the *Son of God, the Sun of Righteousness.*[185] And [11] *Jesus and Samson grew and the Lord blessed them* until the time of their mission.[186]

Temptation of the Deliverer

The Lord's purpose was for Samson to confront the enemy so [12] *the spirit of the LORD began to move him.*[187] Likewise, *Jesus was led up of the Spirit into the wilderness to be tempted of the devil.*[188] [13] **But his father and mother did not [know] that <u>it [was] of the LORD, that he sought an occasion</u>**[189]to confront the enemy. So both were moved by the Spirit and in both cases the Lord sought an occasion for them to confront the enemy. One would confront a physical enemy and the other would confront a supernatural enemy. Samson was driven into the wilderness and was tempted yet *he defeated the roaring lion*, just as Jesus was driven by the Spirit into the wilderness where [14] **Jesus was tempted by Satan, and in the end Jesus defeated Satan, the roaring lion.**[190] Once again the physical events prophetically

---

[183] Judges 13:18.
[184] Judges 13:11, 18.
[185] Malachi 4:2.
[186] Judges 13:24; Luke 1:80.
[187] Judges 13:25; Matthew 4:1.
[188] Matthew 4:1.
[189] Judges 14:4.
[190] Judges 14:5; 1 Peter 5:8.

transform to a supernatural conclusion. Afterwards, both would attend a wedding. [15] **Samson attended the wedding** at Timnath. And Jesus attended **the wedding at Cana.**[191] It was there that Samson gave them [16] the parable of the **change of garments.**[192] And Jesus, likewise gave Nicodemus the **parable of baptism which is the change of garments.** Jesus would have you change your filthy rags for a white robe of righteousness.

Step by step, I could see and hear the events in the life of Samson unfold just as they would in the life of Jesus, hundreds of years into the future. It was becoming clear to me, that the lives of Samson, Joseph, and Isaac were all deliberately choreographed for a purpose. And that purpose was to provide the evidence that would vindicate the character of God the Father which is reflected in His LAW. The underlying encryption was hidden so that those that study[193] would know that God the Father is Love.[194]

Sent them forth Two by Two

As I continued to unlock the encryption, I found that Samson and Jesus were connected by more than 52 points. Samson sent them out [17] **two by two**[195] and [18] **they set the fields on fire** just as Jesus sent the apostles out two by two and **they set the world on fire.** [19] Samson tied the tails of the foxes together and **put a firebrand in the midst of the two tails.** Likewise, Jesus put the Holy Spirit between the two disciples as a firebrand. And you know, that the field is a symbol of the world.[196] Setting the fields on fire [20] **put Samson at war with the enemy.** Likewise, when Jesus sent his apostles into the fields **they went to war against Satan and his fallen demons.** And the disciples *returned again*

---

[191] Judges 14:1-5; John 2:1-10.
[192] Judges 14:12-19.
[193] 2 Timothy 2:15.
[194] 1John 4:16.
[195] Judges 15:4.
[196] Matthew 13:38.

with joy, saying, Lord, even the devils are subject unto us through thy name.[197]

Hip and Thigh

On two separate occasions Samson went into battle with the enemy. [21] In the first engagement, Samson *smote them hip and thigh with a great slaughter.* Hip and thigh takes us back to an earlier passage in the Book of Genesis. Jacob wrestled with the Angel of the Lord until the break of day. And the Angel of the Lord converted Jacob by touching his **thigh**.[198] As you'll recall, Jacob's name which means thief, was changed by the Angel to *Israel, which means overcomer.* Jesus slays the old man within us and we are reborn as overcomers.[199] Jesus converted thousands by giving them rebirth at the feeding of the 5000.[200]

Jawboning is Preaching

After the battle, both Jesus and Samson [22] **rested in the mount.** I see this as far more than coincidence because afterwards [23] **Samson defeated a thousand and Jesus fed the 4000.** [24] **Samson defeated his thousands with the jawbone. Likewise, Jesus preached using His jaw to convert thousands by speaking.** Afterwards Samson, like Jesus [25] **made an end of speaking.**[201] Because Samson, like Jesus, gained the victory[202] over thousands, [26] **the enemy attacked them even more fiercely** than before. Time and again [27] **the enemy plotted to kill both Samson and Jesus and sought a means of** [28] **trapping both of them.** It was then that I realized that the Pharisees were plotting to kill Jesus, just as the Philistines were plotting to kill Samson.

---

[197] Luke 10:17.
[198] Genesis 32:24-32.
[199] 1 John 5:4, 5.
[200] Matthew 14:21.
[201] Judges 15:17.
[202] 1 Corinthians 15:54 – 57.

And it was Jesus that defeated thousands by causing their old selves to perish so that they could be born again. Jesus converted them *by speaking* through the use of his jawbone, just as Samson defeated them physically with the jawbone. And it is most interesting to note that Samson killed them on their hips and thighs. Can you imagine killing a thousand men by hitting their thighs? No! Then why does it make sense? Because it points to the spiritual conversion!

Gates of Hell Shall Not Prevail

After the thousands were slain and converted, both Jesus and Samson went to a place to rest. It was there that both Samson and Jesus were revived. 29 **Samson was revived with the water that came from the jaw.** Jesus **was revived by praying through the Holy Spirit, the water of life.** 30 **Both were compassed about.** 31 It was at that point that **Samson took the Gate of the enemy at midnight and carried it to the top of the Hill.** Likewise, **Jesus took the Gate of hell and began carrying it to Calvary.** Hell means grave, so **Jesus began removing the Gate to the grave to Calvary the night He was compassed about in the Garden of Gethsemane.** Jesus was giving you and I a way of escape from death. *The gates of hell shall not prevail.[203]*

Sold, Captured, and Sacrificed

As I drifted off to sleep, I could almost hear Samson say, **The gates of the city could not contain me.** Likewise, I realized that

---

[203] Matthew 16:18.

the *gates of hell shall not prevail*[204] against Jesus. 32 **Samson, just like Jesus, was sold for silver,** 33 **blinded,** 34 **bound, *and*** 35 **imprisoned**. And in the end, Samson, like Jesus, was seen by the enemy as 36 **a great sacrifice.** 37 Samson and Jesus were both **led like a Lamb to the slaughter.** 38 Both **stretched out their arms before their deaths.** And 39 Both **called upon the Lord for strength.** And in death, 40 **Samson brought down the House of Dagon just as Jesus would bring down the House of Satan, the false god**.

Divinely Intertwined Lives (52!)

The encrypted event sequence in the life of Samson, amazingly reflects 52 events in the life of Jesus, from his birth to his death more than 1000 years before the birth of Jesus. The encryption of 52 parallel events in just 96 verses again is **DELIBERATE**.[205] When you consider the accounts of Joseph and Samson together, the sum of the resulting probability rules out chance. The two accounts are *deliberately encrypted as are those of a great cloud of witnesses*. Together, these witnesses give a much more detailed view of the mission of Jesus. And when these testimonies are considered together with the New Testament, they provide a much more profound understanding of the Plan of Salvation.

As I settled into bed, I couldn't get the code out of my mind. When I realized that the events recorded in the Gospel accounts of the life of Christ are in lock step with the events hidden in the embedded code of numerous Guardians like Joseph, Isaac, and Samson, I had a dilemma. After years of study, I realized that the Code was embedded by a Being or Beings with a view of events outside of time, for they could not only see events in the past but they could see events in the future. And this Being or these Beings are able to interact, influence, and guide the lives of mankind. No matter how I view the Code, I've never been able to come up with an alternative logical explanation. Could the Bible be true?

---

[204] Matthew 16:18.
[205] Alexander, D.H. 2020. The Power of Samson, Guardian of the Code.

Testimony of Samson

He was born when Israel was in captivity
His was a *MIRACLE BIRTH*
His birth was announced by an angel first to his
mother and then to his father
He was Holy and set apart;
the *DELIVERER OF ISRAEL*
His name means "*LIKE THE SUN*"

He was *driven into the wilderness by the Spirit*
There he was tempted and he slayed the roaring lion
He attended the wedding
He gave the parable of the *CHANGE OF GARMENTS*

He *SENT THEM OUT TWO BY TWO* and
THEY SET THE WORLD ON FIRE
Both use the Jawbone to gain the *VICTORY OVER
THOUSANDS ON TWO SEPARATE OCCASIONS*
then he makes an end of speaking
The enemy attacked even more fiercely
They plot to kill him
THE GATES OF HELL CANNOT PREVAIL
He is *SOLD OUT FOR SILVER* and
He is blinded, bound and imprisoned
He is a *GREAT SACRIFICE*

He is led like a lamb to the slaughter
He calls upon the Lord for strength
HE DIES WITH HIS ARMS OUTSTRETCHED
He destroys the house of Dagon the false god

6   3rd Witness: David, King of Kings

Even as David also describeth the blessedness of the man, unto whom God imputeth righteousness without works,   [Saying], Blessed [are] they whose iniquities are forgiven, and whose sins are covered.   Blessed [is] the man to whom the Lord will not impute sin.[206] *These things saith he that is holy, he that is true, he that hath the key of David, he that openeth, and no man shutteth; and shutteth, and no man openeth...*[207]

Looking back, David, the **King of Kings,**[208] carried himself with the regal bearing of one who had overcome many trials and wars. David spoke to the King of the Universe saying, *Who [am] I, O Lord GOD? and what [is] my house, that thou hast brought me hitherto? ... And what can David say more unto thee? for thou, Lord GOD, knowest thy servant. And now, O Lord GOD ... thy words be true, and thou hast promised this goodness unto thy servant...*[209]   King David appears to me now,   far   more impressive   than   I   had

---

[206] Romans 4:6-8.
[207] Revelation 3:7.
[208] Revelation 17:14.
[209] 2 Samuel 7:19-28.

perceived from my superficial readings of the Scriptures. A study of David's account reveals an amazing encryption of the *King of Kings and Lord of Lords.*[210]

Anointed to be King of Israel

King David, like Jesus, was ⑴ **born in Bethlehem** of the ⑵ **lineage of Jesse, the descendant of Boaz, Abraham, and Adam**. The Lord referred to both David and Jesus as His ⑶ "Beloved." David was a ⑷ **good shepherd watching over his father's sheep connecting him to Jesus, the Good Shepherd who tends to the flock of mankind.** The men of Israel crowned Saul for their king, but it was the Lord that ⑸ **crowned David to be the King of Israel** by ⑹ **the hand of the Lord's prophet.** David was but a shepherd boy when the Lord led the prophet to him among the ⑺ **sons of Jesse who was of Obed, the son of Boaz and Ruth.**[211] ⑻ **Then Samuel took the horn of oil, and anointed [him] in the midst of [his] brethren:** *and the* ⑼ **spirit of the LORD came upon [His servant] David, from that day forward.**[212]

The Temptation of 40 Days

David was sent by his father, Jesse, and led by the Spirit to seek his brothers of the army of Israel. Likewise, Jesus was sent by His Father, and led by the Spirit, to go to the people of Israel. ⑽ **Jesus, like David found them at war with the enemy** arrayed on two opposing mountains. The forces David saw, were on physical mountains. Jesus saw the forces arrayed on spiritual mountains. *And the [enemy] stood on a mountain on the one side, and Israel stood on a mountain on the other side:* ⑾ *and* **[there was] a valley between them;**[213] *the* **valley of the shadow of death.**[214]

---

[210] Revelation 17:14; 19:16.
[211] Ruth 4:16-22; Matthew 1:5.
[212] 1 Samuel 16:13.
[213] 1 Samuel 17:3.
[214] Psalm 23:4.

The very same vale that Joseph crossed. The 12 **champion of the enemy was a giant compared to mortal men** and 13 **day in and day out he accused, defied, and tempted the King of Israel** saying, *choose you a man for you, and let him come down to me. If he be able to fight with me, and to kill me, then will we be your servants: but if I prevail against him, and kill him, then shall ye be our servants, and serve us.*[215] He was the 14 **accuser of the brethren**[216] and a 15 **man of war.**[217] The stakes were extremely high for 16 **if the champion of Israel lost, then all of Israel would be enslaved by the enemy**.

It was then that I realized that the childhood story of David and Goliath was far more than a mere child's story. It was the account of the supernatural battle between the armies of Christ and Satan. And David, King of Kings, was the forerunner of Jesus, the very Jesus that would face Satan in the wilderness. I realized that the child David stood before the giant Goliath as Jesus the "man" stood before the fallen angel, Satan. A man is easy prey before an angel but Jesus and David were filled with the Spirit of God. I began to listen intently to every WORD that came out of the mouth of this earthly King. I realized that the war between Jesus and Satan, the two that stood in front of the throne in the heavenly Court, had been repeated over and over again, between the serpent and the Seed of the woman[218] since the beginning of time. I realized that as the two battled one another as the angels that followed Jesus watched from the spiritual mount Zion of heaven. Meanwhile, the fallen demons of Satan watched from the confines of Earth.

I listened to the meaning of the Scriptures more intently as this King David continued staring valiantly at Goliath. 17 The enemy **drew near morning and evening, and presented himself forty days**[219] **just as Satan taunted Jesus in the wilderness 40 days.**

---

[215] 1 Samuel 17:8, 9.
[216] Revelation 12:10.
[217] 1 Samuel 17:33.
[218] Genesis 3:15.
[219] 1 Samuel 17:16.

All Israel feared the enemy and none dared confront him. But David, like Jesus, stepped forward. And David said, [18] **thy servant will go and fight with this Philistine.**[220] But David was told, ***Thou art not able to go against this Philistine to fight with him: for thou [art but] a youth, and he a man of war from his youth.***[221] But David prevailed so that the Lord God should be glorified. Likewise, Jesus stepped forth, a little lower than the angels to confront the mighty angel, Satan.[222]

Yet [19] **when David was given earthly armor he set them aside; just as Jesus set them aside.** ***For we wrestle not against flesh and blood, but against principalities, against powers, against the rulers of the darkness of this world, against spiritual wickedness in high [places]. Wherefore take unto you the whole armor of God, that you may be able to withstand in the evil day... having on the breastplate of righteousness; and your feet shod with the ... gospel of peace; ... taking the shield of faith, ... and ...the helmet of salvation, and the sword of the Spirit, which is the word of God...and for me...that I may open my mouth boldly, to make known the mystery of the gospel...***[223]

David readied himself for battle against Goliath, just as Jesus prepared for battle against the ***old serpent, called the Devil, and Satan, which deceiveth the whole world.***[224] David stopped at a brook that carried the water of life to select 5 well-polished stones. You might say the stones are a piece of [20] **the Rock which is known as the WORD of God.** And David was not afraid, saying [21] **Yea, though I walk through the valley of the shadow of death, I ...fear no evil: for thou [art] with me; thy rod and thy staff they comfort me.**[225] And David took ***the five smooth stones***

---

[220] 1 Samuel 17:32.
[221] 1 Samuel 17:33.
[222] Psalm 8:5; Hebrews 2:7-9.
[223] Ephesians 6:12-20.
[224] Revelation 12:9.
[225] Psalm 23:4.

out of the brook, and put them in a shepherd's bag his sling [was] in his hand: and he drew near to the [enemy].[226]

And the enemy said unto David, *Come to me, and I will give thy flesh unto the fowls of the air, and to the beasts of the field.*[227] And David said, *Thou comest to me with a sword, and with a spear, and with a shield: but I come to thee in the name of the LORD of hosts, the God of the armies of Israel, whom thou hast defied.*[228] *And he took thence a stone, and slang [it], and smote the [enemy] in his forehead, that* 22 **the stone sunk into his forehead;** *and he fell upon his face to the earth and [I] took his sword, and drew it out of the sheath thereof, and slew him, and cut off his head therewith.*[229]

Then I realized that just as 23 **David slew the enemy in the wilderness on the 40**th **day with a well-polished stone, and so would Jesus slay Satan on the 40**th **day** with a well-polished verse of the Rock. The WORD of the Lord, would penetrate the thick skull of the enemy's head. And Jesus would turn the tables on Satan and his followers 24 *saying to all the fowls that fly in the midst of heaven, Come and gather yourselves together unto the supper of the great God; That ye may eat the flesh of kings, and the flesh of captains, and the flesh of mighty men, and the flesh of horses, and*

---

226 1 Samuel 17:40.
227 1 Samuel 17:44; Psalm 79:2.
228 1 Samuel 17:44-45.
229 1 Samuel 17:49-51.

of them that sit on them, and the flesh of all [men, both] free and bond, both small and great. And I saw the beast, and the kings of the earth, and their armies, gathered together to make war against [Jesus] that sat on the horse, and against his army.[230] The final battle between Christ and Satan would be finished at the end of time.

Samson slayed men by using the jawbone slaying thousands hip and thigh. In the parallel, David ☐25 **killed men, removing their foreskins by circumcision**. For this King David said *I arose and went, [with my men], and slew of the [enemy] two hundred men; and [I] brought their foreskins, and they gave them in full tale to the king.*[231] For the cutting off the foreskins represents circumcision and Christ performs *circumcision of the heart, in the spirit, …* For *if any man [be] in Christ, [he is] a new creature: old things are passed away; behold, all things are become new.*[232]

For the next several hours, I heard more than 52 points in the order of King David's life[233] that are in the same order as the events in the life of Jesus more than a thousand years earlier. Both were anointed to be King. Both would overcome the tempter of Israel. Both would defeat the tempter on the 40th day. Both were said to be ☐26 **poor and lightly esteemed**. Both won great victories by circumcision; one of the foreskin and the other of the heart. ☐27 **Both were innocent blood**.[234] Both are destined to become ☐28 **the King of Israel** and referred to as ☐29 the **Angel of God**.[235] Both ☐30 **cared for the lame**. Both are ☐31 **anointed a second time before their deaths**. Both take Zion with a ☐32 **triumphal entry** and reveal themselves as the King of Zion. ☐33 **Their trusted advisors betray them and hang themselves**.[236] ☐34 **Both cross over the**

[230] Revelation 19:17-19.
[231] 1 Samuel 18:27.
[232] Romans 2:29; 2 Corinthians 5:17.
[233] D. H. Alexander. David: King of Kings, Guardian of the Code.
[234] 1 Kings 19:5; Matthew 27:4, 24.
[235] 1 Samuel 29:9; 2 Samuel 14:17, 20; and 19:27;Acts 27:23; Galatians 4:14.
[236] Acts 1:16 tells us that it was the Holy Spirit that guided David's thoughts.

Jordan when 35 **2 swift messengers** (angels) bring 36 **Good**

Testimony of David

He is born in Bethlehem of the lineage of Jesse
His name means **"Beloved"**;
He's the **good shepherd**
God chose him to be King; He is **anointed by the**
prophet and *the Spirit of the Lord enters him*

The Enemy of Israel accused them day and night
If he loses the battle Israel will be enslaved
On the 40TH **DAY** he confronts the enemy
Though small, He is **the chosen** *Champion of Israel*
He defeats the Accuser of the brethren with a rock to
his forehead which is a symbol of the **WORD**

He wins great victories
by *circumcising* those that he confronts
He is wise but **poor and lightly** esteemed
They seek to kill **him yet his** is *innocent blood*

He is destined to become King and
They are referred to as the *Angel of God*
Both care for the lame
Both are anointed a 2nd time as **KING OF ISRAEL;**
Both take the stronghold of Zion and reveal
themselves as King in a **TRIUMPHAL ENTRY.**
His *trusted advisor hangs himself* and the King
crosses over the Jordan but **2 SWIFT MESSENGERS**
bring **GOOD TIDINGS** as
HE crosses back over Jordan

Tidings as they 37 **both go back across the waters of the Jordan!**[237] Yes the two messengers in the account of David point to the two angels that opened the tomb of Jesus!

The Heavenly Court has heard the testimonies of these three witnesses, Joseph, Samson, and David, each faithfully bringing forth the evidence hidden in the accounts of their lives since the foundation of the world. I was now convinced that the evidence was DELIBERATELY hidden. How else could you explain the occurrence of 52 or more events in the same order as the events in the account of Jesus in the lives of multiple independent witnesses. And the accounts of these witnesses were congruent with one another. More amazingly, the accounts of these witnesses were all recorded by different human authors separated by hundreds of years! At the very least, you can be sure that the Bible is a Supernatural Book.

---

[237] 2 Samuel 18:26, 27; Matthew 28:5, 6.

7 4th *Witness: Jonah, Death, Burial, and Resurrection*

For as Jonas was three days and three nights in the whale's belly; so shall the Son of man be three days and three nights in the heart of the earth.[238]

The Lord is willing to go to the ends of the earth and the depths of the seas to rescue the lost, even those that despise Him. For the Lord converted all of Nineveh, the heart of the Assyrian Empire, and the enemies of the Jews, through Jonah, And He accomplished this to demonstrate His immeasurable LOVE. Many look upon Jonah as the reluctant prophet. But nothing is hidden from the eyes of Jesus. For it is Jesus that told the Pharisees that His death, burial, and resurrection was foreshadowed by Jonah's experience with the great sea creature. Jesus told them, *For as Jonas*

---

[238] Matthew 12:40.

was three days and three nights in the whale's belly; so shall the Son of man be three days and three nights in the heart of the earth.[239]   Jesus *spoke to them in parables: because they seeing see not; and hearing they hear not, neither do they understand. And in them is fulfilled the prophecy of Esaias [Isaiah], which saith, By hearing ye shall hear, and shall not understand; and seeing ye shall see, and shall not perceive: For this people's heart is waxed gross, and [their] ears are dull of hearing, and their eyes they have closed.* Had they understood they would not have crucified Jesus. But they proceeded of their own **free will** that the Universe might see how their hearts were poisoned by the Evil One.

Jonah was appropriately named Jonah which means [1] "**Dove**," because his life's record is a shadow of the work of the Holy Spirit in the life of Jesus from His baptism to His ascension. Both [2] are **prophets** and both are [3] **Galileans**.[240] Both [4] **first taught among the Jews** and later both [5] **took the message of salvation to the Gentiles**. When Jonah was [6] **commissioned by God** to take the message of repentance to the Gentiles, [7] Jonah **sped from the presence of the Lord** and [8] entered the vessel, as a shadow of the future when the Dove descended swiftly from the throne of Grace and **entered the living vessel** of Jesus at His baptism.[241]   Both would [9] **pay the price**.

Tempest on the Sea

[10] **Both boarded the ship** and soon [11] **fell asleep**. But once the ship was out upon the sea, [12] **a great tempest arose** and [13] **terrorized the sailors that were with them**. The apostles were experienced mariners, like the brave men that piloted Jonah's ship. Yet in both cases the brave sailors feared for their lives. [14] **The sailors awakened both Jonah and Jesus in hopes that the prophet could calm the storm**. Yet the physical storm was

---

[239] Matthew 12:40.
[240] 2 Kings 14:25. Jonah was of Gaththepher which is of Galilee.
[241] Matthew 3:16, 17.

merely a shadow of the supernatural tempest that fell upon the crowds surrounding the trial of Jesus. For it was Satan that caused the people of the world to cry out for Christ's crucifixion. |15| The **man-in-charge** told both Jonah and Jesus to |16| **call on their God to save themselves** and the crew. In Jonah's case, that man was the Captain of the ship. In Christ's case, that man was called Pilate. Then they |17| **cast lots** in front of Jesus and Jonah. |18| The **lot fell on both Jesus**[242]**and Jonah.**

Tempest on the Sea of Humanity

So |19| **they put them both through a trial**. And the |20| **Man-in-charge questioned them both,** asking: |21| **What is your occupation?** |22| **Where do you come from?** |23| **What is your country?** |24| **What people are you from?** |25| **What shall we do to calm the sea?** |26| **Both Jesus and Jonah are Hebrews who revere the Creator God.**   When the man-in-charge asked them what they needed to do to calm the storm, both told them |27| **they must be sacrificed.** Neither man-in-charge wanted Jesus or Jonah to perish. |28| **They tried to save them from the storm.** But it was of no avail. |29| Then the mariners cried out saying, **let us not perish for this man's sake.** They did not want to bear their |30| **innocent blood**[243]on their consciences, but the storm raged so |31| **they raised both Jesus and Jonah up** and the sea of humanity was quieted and |32| **the storms stopped raging.**

Three Days and Three Nights

As I absorbed Jonah's account, I better understood why Jesus told the Pharisees that He would give them no sign (or miracle) but the Sign of Jonah. **The account of Jonah itself is the miracle.** Yes, the account has numerous miracles within it, but the greatest miracle of all is that the entire account of Jonah is *a prophetic*

---

[242] Matthew 27:17-26. Jonah 1:7.
[243] Jonah 1:14; Matthew 27:24.

foreshadowing and revelation of the events in the life of Jesus, hundreds of years in advance. Jesus said:

> *An evil and adulterous generation seeketh after a sign; and there shall no sign be given to it, but the sign of the prophet Jonas: For as Jonas was three days and three nights in the whale's belly; so shall the Son of man be three days and three nights in the heart of the earth.*[244]

Both are 33 **substitutionary sacrifices**. Jonah's sacrifice would calm the natural waters. Jesus' sacrifice would calm the troubled waters of humanity. 34 **Both willingly gave their lives that others might live.** Both were in the clutches of the 35 **belly of hell**[245] for 36 **three days and three nights**. And 37 **their bodies were both wrapped before they entered their tombs. Jonah was wrapped in seaweed**[246] **as a shadow of Christ's grave clothes.** Yet 38 both of their **bodies escaped corruption**[247] so that the prophecy uttered by the Spirit, through the mouth of David, would be fulfilled. And 39 **Both were resurrected** on the 40 **third day**.

40 Days after the Resurrection

After their resurrection, 41 **both preached for 40 days.** And 42 **both urged the people to repent** and give up their evil ways. And 43 **at the end of the 40 days,** both went to a place on 44 **the east side of the city.** And 45 **the sun did arise** and 46 **many that had been lost, were saved.** And it was the Lord that convicted Jonah to write all these things, that the evidence of Christ's grace might be known to the world.

---

[244] Matthew 12:39, 40.
[245] Johan 2:2.
[246] Jonah 2:5.
[247] Psalm 16:10. Jonah 2:6.

Testimony of Jonah

His name means *"Dove"*

He is a *Prophet of Galilee*; He *preached to the Jews* and *then to the Gentiles*; He sped from the presence of the Lord and entered the vessel to pay the price

There was a *GREAT TEMPEST UPON THE SEA* (of humanity) while he slept as the calm in the eye of the storm; He was commanded to awake and they begged him to pray to his God that they would not perish

They *CAST LOTS* and it fell upon him; and the man in charge *TRIED HIM* asking: Why has this evil fallen upon us?; What is your occupation?; Where do you come from?; What is your country?; What people are you from? What shall we do to calm the Sea(humanity)? He replied: I am a Hebrew. I fear the Creator. If you sacrifice me the Sea will be calmed. The *MARINERS FLED* because his was *INNOCENT BLOOD*. But they *RAISED HIM UP* as a *SUBSTITUTIONARY SACRIFICE* and the sea was calmed and *THE MARINERS FEARED THE LORD GOD*.

A great fish like a tomb, swallowed him up and He was in the belly of hell (the grave) for *3 DAYS AND 3 NIGHTS*. Yet *HIS BODY WAS NOT CORRUPTED RESURRECTED ON THE THIRD DAY*.

FORTY DAYS he preached repentance; said "it is better for me to die than to live." He went to the *East side of the City* and the *Sun did arise* and many were saved.

8 5th *Witness: Elisha, Miracle Worker*

Behold, the child was dead, [and] laid upon his bed. He went in therefore, and shut the door upon them twain, and prayed unto the LORD. And he went up, …and he stretched himself upon the child; and the flesh of the child waxed warm. Then he returned, … and the child opened his eyes… So he called her [the child's mother]. And when she was come in unto him, he said, Take up thy son. Then she went in, and fell at his feet, and bowed herself to the ground, and took up her son, and went out.[248]

Miracles are acts that come from the supernatural. And the Holy Scriptures are themselves Books of miracles, providing a bridge between our natural world and the supernatural. We have discovered that this miraculous bridge connects the natural and supernatural worlds at two or more levels. On the surface, we discover hundreds of

---

[248] 2 Kings 4:32-37; Luke 7:12-15; Matthew 9:18-24.

prophecies of the Old Testament that find their fulfillment in the life of Christ. Below the surface, in the Old Testament, we find accounts of a great cloud of witnesses that also testify of the life of Christ. And all these connections, taken together, were deliberately guided by a Being or Beings that knew the future from the beginning. How else can you explain them, considering that they were written hundreds of years in advance?

As Jesus is the successor to John, so Elisha is the successor to Elijah. Prophets like John the Baptist and Elijah, carried an animal skin as a signature of their profession. The skin is a symbol of sacrifice pointing to Jesus, ***the Lamb slain from the foundation of the world***.[249] It is written, ***For all the prophets and the law prophesied until John. And if ye will receive [it], this is Elias [Elijah], which was for to come***. [250] John the Baptist was a Voice in the wilderness, as was Elijah. Both had a large following of disciples. And Elisha performed twice as many miracles as Elijah. And Jesus performed many more miracles than Elisha.

[1] **The Lord, sent Elijah to anoint Elisha to be a prophet in Israel just as Jesus was anointed by John**. [2] **Both Elijah and John were Nazarites dedicated to the Lord.** Both were hairy men, girt with a girdle of leather about their loins. They preceded Elisha and Jesus to clear the way for ministries that would lead men to salvation. [3] Importantly, **the given names of Elisha and Jesus share the same meaning: "God is Salvation."** Their names were not given to them by accident.

Elijah came to Elisha as [4] **he labored with the 12, just as John came to Jesus as He labored with the 12.** [5] **The prophet led Elisha to the Jordan just as John the Baptist led Jesus to the Jordan**. And there, Elisha requested a [6] **double portion of the spirit**. And a ***double portion*** fell upon Elisha just as it did on Jesus. The [7] **mantle of Elijah fell and the spirit descended upon Elisha from heaven**[251] **just as the dove descended upon**

[249] Revelation 13:8.
[250] Matthew 11:13, 14.
[251] 2 Kings 2:15.

Jesus. You might say Jesus had a double portion of the Trinity to carry out His ministry. Likewise, Elisha received a double portion and 9 **performed twice as many miracles as Elijah. Yet the portion poured upon Jesus was far greater than that poured out on Elisha.** Both 10 **grieved at the passing of their predecessors after their experience at the Jordan.** Following the Jordan experience, in which the waters from below and those above were parted, 11 **both took the disciples of their forerunner under their wings.** 12 **Both healed the waters of the city.** Elisha healed the waters of the city with salt and he healed the land from death. Jesus healed the people of the city with His life-giving waters through His disciples, the salt of the earth, and healed the world from death.

The children of 13 **Israel made fun of both of Elisha and Jesus because of their talk of the ascension.**[252] 14 **Both warned the King of Israel and the leadership to turn back to the prophecies of the prophets of old**, for the answers they sought were hidden there.[253]

In one place it is written, 15 **the creditor came to take away the woman's children just as Satan came to steal the souls of the children of Israel.** But 16 **Elisha multiplied the oil in the empty vessels just as Jesus multiplied the Holy Spirit in the vessels of the people of Israel.** 17 **The oil was used by the woman to pay the debt, just as the Holy Spirit led the lost to pay their debts of sin by seeking forgiveness through Jesus, our Lord.**

In another place it is written that **there was a young man that was with the reapers and he later died upon his mother's lap.** 18 **As was the case of Mary and Lazarus, the woman was certain that Elisha could use the powers given him to raise the child from the dead.** 19 **Elisha tarried until the boy was dead, just as Jesus waited until Lazarus was dead.** 20 **Both tarried to demonstrate the resurrecting power of God.** After waiting to

---

[252] 2 Kings 2:23.
[253] 2 Kings 3:13.

assure that the child was dead, Elisha went to the woman's house and lay upon the boy and his life was restored. **Like Elisha, Jesus tarried so that the Father that sits on the throne might be glorified with His life giving power** for it is from Him that Jesus had power to raise the dead. Jesus then went to raise Lazarus. 21 **The resurrection of these two young men was granted because of the faith of the two women.**

In yet another place, 22 **Elisha multiplied the food for a hundred men and later Jesus fed the 4000 and the 5000. The miracles of Jesus were far greater than the prophets that preceded Him.**

In another place the Scriptures tell of 23 **the healing of the leper.** Elisha caused the leper to submerge himself 7 times in the Jordan and he was clean. And there is a hidden message in this! Seven is the number of completeness. 24 When the leper totally believed in the miracle, he was cleansed. And **Jesus cleansed many lepers because of their belief.** The healing of Jesus was complete. Both Elisha and Jesus were 25 **betrayed by their servants for the lust of money.** 26 **Both were given bags of silver** to satisfy their personal greed. Gehazi brought shame on himself pointing to the time when Judas would do the same. And in the end 27 **both were cursed** with the sickness[254] of their sins. And then there is 28 **the resurrection power of the tombs of Elisha**[255] **and Jesus.**

Harmony of the Types

The miracles of Elisha were two-fold those of Elijah. But both were far exceeded by the miracles performed by Jesus. As I reflected on the testimonies of Joseph, Isaac, Samson, David, Jonah, and Elisha I began to realize that each held a piece of the puzzle that is fully realized in Jesus. The pieces fit together congruently and their logic is internally consistent. More importantly, when they are compared, they reveal a much deeper understanding of the Plan of Salvation and the loving character of

---

[254] 2 Kings 5:27.
[255] 2 Kings 13:21.

our God. It is through this Harmony of the Types that one gains a much deeper understanding of Jesus and the Plan of Salvation. I realize now, that none can adequately appreciate the depth and breadth of the Plan of Salvation without comparing the hidden evidence of the Old Testament with the New Testament.

The Old Testament is Christ concealed.
The New Testament is Christ revealed.

Divinely Intertwined Lives (52!)

The encrypted event sequence in the lives of Joseph, Samson, David, Elisha, and Jonah each reflect more than 52 events in the same order that they would later be manifested in the life of Jesus hundreds of years into the future. The same Angel of the Lord that announced the birth of Samson, the very same One that spoke words through the mouth of David, is the very same Jesus that can bring you back from the dead. Jesus stands, even now, as your Counsellor before the Court of Heaven making intercession for your salvation.

The ENCRYPTED SEQUENCE of EVENTS of more than 52 points in the same order as those in the life of Christ, in each of the five independent accounts is such an incredible probability that it has to be DELIBERATE! The fact that their event sequences are all consistent with one another, and with the life of Christ, can only be explained as having been orchestrated by an Author outside of time. The Bible claims that its authors are guided by the Holy Spirit of God. How else could all of this have been known in advance?

Testimony of Elisha

The Lord sent the prophet to Select his Successor
Elijah and John were both Nazarites
Their names mean **"GOD IS SALVATION"**
John is the Elijah to come; John and Elijah call the
people to repent; Elisha and Jesus come to save
He labors with the 12
**PROPHET LEADS HIM TO THE JORDAN; BOTH
RECEIVE A DOUBLE PORTION; THEY GRIEVE
THE LOSS OF THE PROPHET**
They accumulate more disciples than their
predecessors; Salt heals the waters of the city; just as
Jesus heals with life-giving waters
They mock their belief in the Ascension;

The creditor (Satan) comes to take the children slaves
SETS THEM FREE BY MULTIPLYING THE OIL
Oil (Holy Spirit) for the woman (the church)
A young man was with the reapers (fallen angels)
when he dies. They delay coming until the young
man's death is complete; **THE WOMAN HAS FAITH
THAT HE CAN BRING HIM BACK TO LIFE;
HE RESURRECTS THE DEAD**

Servants protest that there is not enough food to feed
so many; **MULTIPLIES THE FOOD** and there is food
left over; **HEALS THE LEPER
BETRAYED BY SERVANT FOR LUST OF SILVER**

HIS TOMB BRINGS BACK LIFE TO THE DEAD

9 6th *Witness: Moses, The Deliverer*

By faith Moses, when he was come to years, refused to be called the son of Pharaoh's daughter; Choosing rather to suffer affliction with the people of God... Esteeming the reproach of Christ greater riches than the treasures in Egypt: for he had respect unto the recompense of the reward. By faith he forsook Egypt, not fearing the wrath of the king: for he endured, as seeing him who is invisible.[256]

Satan is the very enemy that caused the war in heaven. He is the very same one that caused mankind to fall through a sinister plot to take over the universe. He is the very same enemy that confronted Israel in Egypt. He is the one that confronted Israel in the wilderness for forty years and opposed Jesus in the wilderness for forty days. It was Satan that caused Pharaoh to charge *all his people, saying, Every son that is born ye shall cast into the river, and every daughter ye shall save*

---

[256] Hebrews 11:23-27.

alive.[257]   And he is the very same murderer recorded by John which says, **the dragon stood before the woman which was ready to be delivered, for to devour her child as soon as it was born. And she brought forth a man child, who was to rule all nations with a rod of iron...**[258]

His Miraculous Birth

I soon realized that Satan was so power hungry that he would stop at nothing to maintain control of his earthly kingdom.   Satan studied the 400 year time prophecy[259] given to Abraham and he was certain that that Seed of the woman would Deliver mankind in the days of the birth of Moses.   Satan would stoop to the lowest imaginable level of morale depravity, even causing the slaying of innocent babies and children to maintain control of planet Earth.

It would have been easy for Satan to confuse the birth of Moses for the birth of Jesus. Moses was 1 **born while Israel was held in bondage.** The 2 **births of Jesus and Moses were miracles** and their births came at a time when 3 **talk of a Deliverer abounded.**[260]   At their births Satan, the force behind the ruler of the land 4 **issued a decree to kill the children in hopes of eliminating the Deliverer.** Like Jesus, Moses was 5 **given refuge in Egypt** so that it might be said of him and of Jesus, 6 **Out of Egypt have I called my son.**[261] And 7 they **both grew in Egypt.** Both were 8 **destined to be second to the throne**[262] and 9 both **were adopted sons.** Moses was the adopted son of the king's daughter,[263] just as Jesus was an adopted son of Joseph. And both loved their brethren so much, that 10 **they were willing to leave**

---

[257] Exodus 1:22.
[258] Revelation 12:4, 5. Exodus 1:22; Matthew 2:16-18. Jeremiah 31:15.
[259] Genesis 15:13; Exodus 12:40-41; Galatians 3:16, 17.
[260] Genesis 15:13; Acts 7:6; Galatians 3:17.
[261] Exodus 13:8; Hosea 11:1; Matthew 2:15.
[262] Hebrews 12:2.
[263] Exodus 2:10.

their thrones choosing rather to suffer affliction with the people of God.

From the days of the Garden, to the days of Jesus, Satan is the one that sought to kill Jesus,[264] our Deliverer. Satan causes evil among men by using false accusations. But 11 **God prepared the Deliverer a way of escape that the testimony might be preserved and written in advance.** 12 **The Lord prepared an ark**[265] **for Noah and an Ark**[266] **for Moses. Moses' Ark was to be the pattern of the Ark of the Testimony**[267] **not made with man's hands.**[268] **All three arks provide a way of escape.**

The Women at the Well

As I listened to the written testimony of Moses, I was now certain that the events in the lives of these Guardians was the physical manifestation of the parallel unseen supernatural events in the war between Christ and Satan. Events in the lives of selected Guardians are provided as evidence, foreshadowing the events in the life of Jesus. But they are also deployed as a means of explaining to mankind the events of the supernatural war between the forces of Christ and Satan, in simplified terms that we can understand. I wondered what the next events would be in the life of Moses that pointed to those in the earthly walk of Jesus. I listened all the more intently as I read the Scriptures.

Moses 13 **intervened to protect his brethren that were held in slavery**, just as Jesus intervened to help mankind by freeing them from illness and demons that held them in spiritual slavery. Moses fled from Egypt and entered the land of Midian of the 14 gentiles as **a stranger in a strange land**[269] just as Jesus later took His ministry to the land of the gentiles. Moses was athirst and he

---

[264] Matthew 2:16-18. Jeremiah 31:15. Genesis 3:15, Genesis 4:8.

[265] Genesis 6:14-19.

[266] Exodus 2:3.

[267] Exodus 25:16-22; Joshua 4:16; Revelation 11:19.

[268] Hebrews 9:11. 24.

[269] Exodus 2:22.

sought water and he found women at a well that *drew [water], and filled the troughs to water their father's flock. And the shepherds came and drove them away: but [I] Moses stood up and helped them, and watered their flock.*[270] |15| **Moses met the women at the well to point, more than a thousand years in advance, to Jesus' meeting with the woman at the well** so that mankind might know that Jesus is the source of living water *springing up into everlasting life.* Was it not |16| **Jesus that sat at the well and rescued the woman and her company in the strange land of the gentiles?** And was not the water that sprung from His side on the Cross, the water of eternal life?[271]

His Commission and Miracles

I realized that *all these things happened unto them for ensamples: and they are written for our admonition, upon whom the ends of the world are come.*[272]   It was Jesus that created the Earth,[273] it was Jesus that formed Adam,[274] it was Jesus that spoke with Noah,[275] it was Jesus that gave the Promise to Abraham[276] and met with Abraham and Sarah face to face,[277] it was Jesus that sought the release of Israel through the mighty works wrought through Moses and Aaron, and this Jesus was the very One that personally announced the births of Isaac[278] and Samson.[279]

Moses shepherded his flock in the darkness of the land of the gentiles. And it was there that |17| **Moses saw a Great Light.**[280] And that Light was the light of the Angel of the Lord known as the

[270] Exodus 2:17-19.
[271] John 4:5-30.
[272] 1 Corinthians 10:11.
[273] Hebrews 1:2.
[274] Genesis 1:26; 2:21-23.
[275] Genesis 6:13.
[276] Genesis 12:7; 15:4,5.
[277] Genesis 17:15-21; 18:1-15.
[278] Genesis 18:10.
[279] Judges 13:18.
[280] Isaiah 9:2; Matthew 4:16.

I AM THAT I AM.[281]   The Angel of the Lord gave Moses the $\boxed{18}$ **commission to be the Deliverer of God's people.**[282]   Jesus is the very same Angel of the Lord, that worked many miracles through Moses as if Moses were $\boxed{19}$ **a prophet.** And it is the Spirit of Jesus that worked through Moses, just as He worked through David;[283] Jesus is the true Prophet.   For it is of Jesus that Moses said to the people of Israel, ***The LORD thy God will raise up unto thee a Prophet from the midst of thee, of thy brethren, like unto me; unto him ye shall hearken...***[284] And Jesus later said, ***father Abraham rejoiced to see my day: and he saw [it], and was glad... Verily, verily, I say unto you, Before Abraham was, I AM.***[285]

It was $\boxed{20}$ **through the rod**[286] **that Jesus worked miracles** in front of the rulers of the world. $\boxed{21}$ **Both Moses and Jesus were confirmed as Deliverers of Israel through many miracles.** And Jesus, was the Angel of the Lord that gave the power to Moses for the miracles he worked.   As $\boxed{22}$ **Moses delivered Israel from slavery**, so too does Jesus perform many miracles and delivers mankind from the slavery of sin.   The $\boxed{23}$ miracles performed before Pharaoh, show the great **power of Jesus over the god's of this world that hold Israel in bondage.**   Satan and his demons performed miracles but they were far inferior to the miracles wrought by Jesus.   The miracles of Jesus were more powerful than those of the serpent[287] for Jesus drove out many demons.[288] $\boxed{24}$ Both Moses and Jesus performed **miracles that overcame disease**, and $\boxed{25}$ **showed power over nature.**   Just as $\boxed{26}$ **Moses delivered Israel from bondage, so too does Jesus lead spiritual Israel**[289] **from the bondage of sin.**   All the mighty acts that were wrought in Egypt and the wilderness were but physical acts pointing to the Spiritual victories that God works for spiritual Israel through Jesus.

---

[281] Exodus 3:2-22. John 8:58.
[282] Hebrews 1:1.
[283] Acts 1:16.
[284] Deuteronomy 18:15; Acts 3:22-26.
[285] John 8:56-58.
[286] Exodus 7:9, 12, 19, 20; Revelation 2:27; 12:5; 19:15.
[287] Exodus 7:9, 10; Revelation 12:9.
[288] Mark 5:9-16.
[289] 1 Peter 2:5.

Paul said, *Moreover, brethren, I would not that ye should be ignorant, how that all our fathers were under the cloud, and all passed through the sea;* |27| **And were all baptized unto Moses in the cloud and in the sea;** |28| **And did all eat the same spiritual meat;** *And* |29| *did all drink the same spiritual drink: for they drank of that spiritual Rock that followed them: and that Rock was Christ.*[290] |30| **Both Jesus and Moses led Israel across the Red Sea and** |31| **through the wilderness** because Jesus was the Angel in the pillar cloud.[291] And it was this same Jesus that spoke to Moses from the cloud.[292]

Renewed Covenant Ministry

This is the same Jesus that led Israel through the Wilderness of Sin, just as He leads His people today through the wilderness of sin. It was there that |32| **Jesus performed the miracle of the manna from heaven, just as He multiplies the bread for His people, even today.** But in TRUTH it is Jesus Himself who is the |33| manna which is the Bread of Heaven.[293] Jesus said, *Verily, verily, I say unto you, Moses gave you not that bread from heaven; but my Father giveth you the true bread from heaven. For the bread of God is he which cometh down from heaven, and giveth life unto the world.*[294] |34| **Jesus multiplied the bread and when they collected it, there was more remaining than when they began** which is a metaphor for the WORD of God, the Bread of Life. In TRUTH, when you digest His WORD, the more you eat, the more that remains! It is the WORD without end!

And the same can be said of the miracle of the water that Jesus provided them in the wilderness,[295] |35| for **the water came out**

---

[290] 1 Corinthians 10:1-4.

[291] Exodus 13:21-22; 14:9;

[292] Exodus 33:11; Numbers 12:5-8.

[293] Exodus 16:4; Psalm 105:40;

[294] John 6:32, 33; 6:50-58.

[295] Exodus 17:6; Numbers 20:8-11.

abundantly, and the congregation drank.[296] Jesus said, ***Whosoever drinketh of this water shall thirst again: But whosoever drinketh of the water that I shall give him shall never thirst; but the water that I shall give him shall be in him a well of water springing up into everlasting life.***[297] Moses, like Jesus, gave the people a ⃞36 **sermon from the Mount.**[298] Like Jesus, Moses ⃞37 **sent forth the 12**[299] into the unchartered lands. And just like Jesus, ⃞38 **Moses selected 70**[300] of the elders of Israel to worship in the Mount.

Intercession and Transfiguration

Who [is] he that condemneth? [It is] Christ that died, yea rather, that is risen again, who is even at the right hand of God, who also maketh intercession for us.[301] And ⃞39 was it not **Moses, like Jesus, that interceded for the people** just as Jesus does even to this day? Did Moses not say ***LORD, why doth thy wrath wax hot against thy people, which thou hast brought forth out of the land of Egypt with great power, and with a mighty hand? ... Remember Abraham, Isaac, and Israel, thy servants, to whom thou swarest by thine own self, and saidst unto them, I will multiply your seed as the stars of heaven, and all this land that I have spoken of will I give unto your seed, and they shall inherit [it] forever. And the LORD repented of the evil which he thought to do unto his people.***[302] And the skin of Moses face shone after being in the presence of Jesus on the Mount. And later, Moses was ⃞40 **transfigured** with Jesus before His followers ***and his face did shine as the sun, and his raiment was white as the light.***[303] And when Moses met Jesus on the mount, is it not recorded, ***the children of Israel saw the face of Moses, that the skin of Moses'***

---

[296] Numbers 20:11.
[297] John 4:13, 14.
[298] Exodus 25:2 and 35:1.
[299] Numbers 17:2, 6; Deuteronomy 1:23; Matthew 10:1.
[300] Exodus 24:1, 9. Luke 10:1, 17.
[301] Romans 8:34.
[302] Exodus 32:11-14.
[303] Matthew 17:2.

face shone: and Moses put the veil upon his face again, until he went in to speak with him.[304] Moses was a forerunner of Jesus seeing that both Jesus and Moses interceded for the people and were transfigured by His Light. Yet Moses is but one among a great cloud of witnesses that testify of Him.[305]

Power of the Cross

The attack of serpents in the wilderness foreshadows Satan's deadly bite of sin. Jesus allowed this to foreshadow the Cross. For it was in the wilderness that Jesus said unto Moses 41 **Make thee a fiery serpent, and set it upon a pole: and it shall come to pass, that every one that is bitten, when he looketh upon it, shall live.**[306] You see, sin is the deadly bite of the serpent because *the wages of sin [is] death; but the gift of God [is] eternal life through Jesus Christ our Lord.*[307] For Jesus said to Nicodemus that as *Moses lifted up the serpent in the wilderness, even so must the Son of man be lifted up: That whosoever believeth in him should not perish, but have eternal life.*[308]

Resurrection

Jesus said, *If they hear not Moses and the prophets, neither will they be persuaded, though one rose from the dead.*[309] For many have read the writings of Moses and yet they still don't believe, even though Jesus raised Lazarus from the dead. Moses was also 42 **resurrected** by Jesus for it is recorded that *Michael the archangel, when contending with the devil he disputed about the body of Moses, durst not bring against him a railing accusation, but said, The Lord rebuke thee.*[310] And Jesus Himself was

---

[304] Exodus 34:34, 35.
[305] Hebrews 12:1.
[306] Numbers 21:8.
[307] Romans 6:23.
[308] John 3:14, 15.
[309] Luke 16:31.
[310] Jude 1:9.

resurrected from the dead. After all, Moses and Elijah counseled and encouraged Jesus on the mount of Christ's Transfiguration.

Supernaturally Connected

The Word of God is designed to captivate our senses. And it is mysteriously effective in reaching the heart. It's like a Physician's scalpel, *sharper than any two-edged sword, piercing even to the dividing asunder of soul and spirit, and of the joints and marrow, and [is] a discerner of the thoughts and intents of the heart.*[311] The events in the lives of all of the Guardians point to events in the life of Jesus. Again, I have documented 52 events in the life of Moses that prefigured 52 events in the life of Jesus in order from their births to the Cross and resurrection. Yet what I present is but a small sample of the overwhelming evidence that the Scriptures were written with the guidance of a Supernatural Being that we refer to as the Holy Spirit.

---

[311] Hebrews 4:12.

Testimony of Moses

He is born when **ISRAEL IS IN BONDAGE**
His is a miracle birth; At his birth
DECREE TO KILL ALL MALE CHILDREN;
He is given refuge in Egypt and he is an adopted son;
and He is **SON OF THE MOST HIGH**
Defeats the Egyptian; A Stranger to the Gentiles;
SAVES WOMEN AT THE WELL.
He becomes a Good Shepherd
Sees a **GREAT LIGHT** and is given a
COMMISSION TO DELIVER ISRAEL
from bondage by the I AM THAT I AM;

His **MISSION CONFIRMED BY MIRACLES**; He has
miraculous **POWER OVER THE SERPENT AND
DISEASE**. He warns of judgments but rulers scoff at
him; He has power over nature and leads Israel in
baptism through the water.
**MIRACLE OF BREAD FOR THE MULTITUDES
MIRACLE OF LIVING WATER FOR MULTITUDES**
He is given a new covenant and
gives a **SERMON FROM THE MOUNT**;

He **SENDS FORTH THE 12 AND ELECTS 70**

INTERCEDES FOR THE PEOPLE;
MEETS GOD FACE TO FACE;
TRANSFIGURED ON THE MOUNT with face aglow
Lifts up **THE CROSS AS THE ANTIDOTE FOR SIN**
He is **RESURRECTED** and fought over by Satan

10   7th *Witness: Joshua, Deliverance*

When ye see the ark of the covenant of the LORD your God, and the priests the Levites bearing it, then ye shall remove from your place, and go after it. Yet there shall be a space between you and it, <u>about two thousand</u> cubits by measure: come not near unto it, that ye may know the way by which ye must go: <u>for ye have not passed [this] way heretofore</u>...And as they that bare the ark were come unto Jordan...the waters which came down from above stood [and] rose up upon an heap very far from the city <u>Adam</u>, ... and those that came down toward the sea of the plain, [even] the salt sea [Dead Sea], failed, [and] were cut off...[312]

Moses left Israel at the edge of the Promised Land like the cliffhanger of a novel. How could the Law of Moses, referred to as the Torah, end without the completion of God's mission? <u>The final acts of the Plan of Salvation</u> are ingeniously choreographed through the book of Joshua, the sequel to the Torah. It is apparent that the author of the Scriptures goes to great lengths to communicate with His people. God uses the lives of men to help explain the

[312] Joshua 3:4, 15, 16.

97

unexplainable. Through the lives of such a great cloud of witnesses, God paints images in terms that humankind can understand, connecting our understanding with the realm of the unseen world of the supernatural. Yet, how does God help us understand the mission of both the Jesus that walked the earth and the Jesus that is now in the Holiest Place in heaven interceding for us?

Supernaturally Connected

In order to enable humankind to understand the role of Jesus from His earthly walk to His heavenly walk, we are provided a bridge that connects them through two characters. Specifically, the life of David represents the earthly walk of Jesus from His birth in Bethlehem and David's son Solomon represents the heavenly Judge of Israel. Likewise, Moses documents the steps taken during Christ's life on Earth, from His birth to His death. The events in the account of Joshua point to the events in Christ's ministry in the heavenly Sanctuary from His ascension, His Second Coming, the destruction of the wicked, and the Kingdom inheritance of the people. Together, Moses and Joshua faithfully walk together through the Plan of Salvation, step-by-step. After Moses died, Joshua completed the work. **Joshua is the** $\boxed{1}$ **successor of Moses** just as **the Comforter is Christ's successor**. Moses was given the mission to illustrate the earthly walk of Christ. Joshua was given the mission to $\boxed{2}$ **guide the people home to the Promised Land**.

In the days of Moses, *before faith came, we were kept under the law, shut up unto <u>the faith which should afterwards be revealed</u>. Wherefore, the law was our schoolmaster [to bring us] unto Christ, that we might be justified by faith.[313]* Of a certainty, *All these things happened unto them for ensamples: and they are written for ... admonition, upon whom the ends of the world are come.[314]* Numerous events in the life of Moses have been fulfilled during the earthly walk of Jesus as recorded in the four Gospels.

---

[313] Galatians 3:23, 24.
[314] 1 Corinthians 10:11.

But now that Jesus has entered into the heavenly Sanctuary, we turn to Joshua to see into the future. Already the world is going through End Time events that are faithfully displayed in the life of Joshua, thousands of years in advance. As surely as every past event pertaining to the life of Christ has been fulfilled, so too will every future event unfold just as it is recorded in the account of Joshua (and others like Joseph). Jesus is working even now to take His people home across the Jordan to the heavenly Canaan.

Innumerable past events have been fulfilled by the earthly walk of Jesus. Joseph descended from the beautiful Canaan, a figure of Heaven, just as Jesus descended from Heaven itself at His birth in Bethlehem to seek the lost sheep of Israel. Events in the lives of Joseph and the other witnesses including Isaac, Samson, David, Elisha, Jonah, and Moses were used by the Spirit to pen the events of Christ's earthly walk in great detail, hundreds of years in advance, so that there would be no doubt that Jesus is a God of LOVE. Jesus *was made a little lower than the angels for the suffering of death, crowned with glory and honour; that ... by the grace of God [He] should taste death for every man.*[315]

Future events, are likewise being fulfilled, step-by-step, in accordance with the records of the Guardians. Numerous accounts like those of Joseph, Joshua, Boaz, Ezekiel, the Revelation of John, and especially the Sanctuary pattern, faithfully point to End Time events. Joseph's life resulted in a great deliverance; the life of Jesus will result in a far greater deliverance. Unto Jesus, as with Joseph, shall the gathering of the people be. Joseph's gathering represents a large number of people, but Christ's gathering will be a *great multitude, which no man could number, of all nations, and kindreds, and people, and tongues.*[316] **Joshua's account outlines events that take us from the ascension of Christ from the Mount of Olives to the end of the Revelation of John.** Jesus, like Boaz is our kinsman Redeemer.

---

[315] Hebrews 2:9.
[316] Revelation 7:9.

Joshua Reveals End Time Events

Joshua's name means ③ **Jehovah Saves, Savior, or Deliverer**. Joshua is the **son of Nun**, whose name means ④ **posterity or eternity**. You might say that Joshua's name, like the name of Jesus, means ⑤ **Savior, Son of Eternity**. Joshua was a priest in the earthly sanctuary, and Jesus is a High Priest of the order of *Melchisedec,* which is of a priesthood *of a better testament.*[317]

Joshua accompanied Moses across the Red Sea which is ⑥ **a figure of baptism**. Joshua witnessed many of the Lord's miraculous works including the opening of the Red Sea. Joshua was of the ⑦ **twelve selected by** Moses and ⑧ he was **sent out two by two**. Likewise, Jesus selected twelve apostles and sent them out two by two. When Israel arrived in Rephidim, ⑨ Joshua **fought the enemy at the foot of the Mount**[318] while Moses ⑩ **held his hands outstretched**. The events at Rephidim were ⑪ **a figure of the battle that was later fought at the foot of the Cross,** when Jesus stretched out his hands to save mankind. In those hours, Satan riled the crowd as they shouted *Crucify Him! Crucify Him!*[319] Joshua was a servant of Moses and together they ⑫ **climbed the Mount of God**[320] just as Jesus ascended the Mount with the Holy Spirit to be with His Father. Moses and Joshua were on the Mount ⑬ **40 days and 40 nights** just as Jesus was in the wilderness 40 days and 40 nights. It was in the wilderness that Moses was given the LAW and the pattern of the sanctuary.[321] And it was there that the Lord made a covenant with Moses saying, *Write thou these words: for after the tenor of these words I have made a covenant with thee and with Israel.*[322]

---

[317] Hebrews 7:22.
[318] Numbers 17:8-16.
[319] Mark 15:13, 14.
[320] Exodus 24:13.
[321] Exodus 25:9.
[322] Exodus 34:27, 28.

Priest of the Sanctuary

Joshua was appointed as a 14 **priest in the earthly tabernacle**[323] just as Jesus was appointed to be High Priest[324] in the heavenly sanctuary. The earthly tabernacle is a pattern of the heavenly tabernacle.[325] Joshua was a 15 **minister**[326] *of the* 16 **sanctuary** just as Jesus is *a minister of the sanctuary and the true tabernacle, which the Lord pitched, and not man.*[327] The events of the early life of Joshua were earthly, yet each step pointed to events in the movements of Jesus in the invisible world of Heaven.

After Moses and Joshua returned from 40 days upon the Mount they heard 17 **trouble in the camp.** When Moses *saw the calf, and the dancing: and Moses'* 18 **anger waxed hot, and he** 19 **threw down the tables** out of his hands, and brake them beneath the mount.**[328] The scene provoked Moses to wrath because the people were trampling the LAW beneath their feet. Similarly, when Jesus began His public ministry, He was likewise provoked to wrath[329] because of the defilement of the temple. When Jesus entered the temple *He threw down the tables* and cleansed the temple from blasphemy and desecration of God's Holy temple and LAW. Joshua was 20 **anointed by the prophet**[330] just as Jesus was anointed by the prophet.

Two Messengers before Crossing

Before Israel crossed the Jordan, the Lord commanded Joshua saying, *this book of the law shall not depart out of thy mouth; but thou shalt meditate therein day and night, that thou mayest*

---

[323] Exodus 33:11; Hebrews 3:1.
[324] Hebrews 6:20.
[325] Hebrews 8:5.
[326] Exodus 24:13.
[327] Hebrews 8:2.
[328] Exodus 32:19.
[329] Mark 11:15-17.
[330] Deuteronomy 31:14; 34:9,10.

observe to do all that is written therein.[331] 21 So from that day forward Joshua, like Jesus, **meditated upon the Book of the Law day and night.** And 22 **God was with Joshua, as God was with Moses, and would later be with Jesus** 23 saying, **I will not fail thee, nor forsake thee.**[332] And Joshua, like Jesus, 24 **sent out messengers to the land of the lost.** And 25 **the messengers gave a warning to the people** that Jericho would soon fall to the Creator God with the power over the waters.[333] And 26 Israel also **gave a promise that those with the red cord would be saved.**[334] And the Angel Messenger of Jesus says, *Fear God, and give glory to him; for the hour of his judgment is come and worship him that made heaven, and earth, and the sea, and the fountains of waters.*[335] And the Angel would also say, *come out of her, my people, that ye be not partakers of her sins, and that ye receive not of her plagues.* Those with Christ's blood on their hearts shall be spared.

Washing Away the Sins of Israel

The day came when the people would cross the Jordan. It would be another ensample, a pattern of future events. It would be a grand enactment of the Plan of Salvation. It would point to the events that would confront those of us in the End of Time.

The Lord ordered the people saying *When ye see the ark of the covenant of the LORD your God, and the priests the Levites bearing it, then ye shall remove from your place, and go after it* leaving *a space between you and it, about two thousand...come not near unto it, that ye may know the way by which ye must go: for ye have not passed [this] way heretofore.*[336] And the priests bearing the ark shall stand still in Jordan.[337] 27 In like manner,

---

[331] Joshua 1:8.
[332] Joshua 1:5.
[333] Joshua 2:10.
[334] Joshua 2:18.
[335] Revelation 14:7; 18:4.
[336] Joshua 3:3, 4.
[337] Joshua 3:8.

Jesus Crossed over the Jordan long before the gathering of His people to prepare a place for them. They shall follow in His footsteps by **2000**. For it is written, *the LORD of all the earth passeth over before you into Jordan*.[338] At the death of Christ, it is written, *the Lord of all the earth, shall rest in the waters of Jordan.* [339] And *the waters of Jordan shall be cut off [from] the waters that come down from above; and they shall stand upon an heap[340] just as Jesus would later be cut-off.* And the cleansing waters of the Jordan shall go all the way back to 28 **Adam** and the sins of all the people of Israel shall be carried to the 29 **Dead Sea**[341] for the wages of sin [is] death. 30 And all of **Christ's people must pass in judgment before the Ark of the Covenant** as in the Day of Atonement[342] that their 31 sins may be washed away.[343] And as it was in the days of Joshua, so shall it be in the time of the end, for 32 **the reproach of Egypt will be rolled away** from Israel.[344]

Israel constructed a memorial on the far side of the Jordan after they crossed the Jordan. Joshua directed each tribe to send a representative to take a stone from the place where the priests held the ark. The stones represent 33 **the cleansed hearts** of each of the twelve tribes *that Crossed before the ark by the living water of Jesus.*[345] *After Israel crossed the Jordan, the LORD said... make thee sharp knives, and circumcise again the children of Israel the second time.*[346] And Joshua made *sharp knives, and circumcised the children of Israel at the hill of the foreskins. Wherefore, the name of the place is called Gilgal unto this day.* Gilgal means Golgotha in the Syriac language. 34 **Symbolically the people of Israel must stand before the Cross and undergo**

---

[338] Joshua 3:11.
[339] Joshua 3:13.
[340] Joshua 3:13.
[341] Joshua 3:16.
[342] Leviticus 16:1-34; 16:30-34; 23:27; 25:9.
[343] Joshua 3:17; 4:1.
[344] Joshua 5:9; (reproach or disgrace).
[345] Joshua 4:8.
[346] Joshua 5:2, 3.

the circumcision of the heart[347] after they pass before the ark of the covenant at the crossing of the Jordan.

End of Probation

Israel observed the Passover on the 14th day of the 1st month[348] just as the Lord had commanded Moses to do. 35 The **celebration of the Passover** was followed by the 36 **feast of unleavened bread**[349] and 37 they ate of the **first fruits**[350] of the land that year. These three feasts commemorated the Exodus from Egypt and again pointed to the crucifixion, burial, and resurrection of Jesus hundreds of years into the future.[351] *Now Jericho was straitly shut up because of the children of Israel:* 38 **none went out, and none came in.**[352] This points to the time when *no man was able to enter into the temple*[353] *of Heaven* signifying that probation is closed. Thereafter, Jesus appeared to Joshua near Jericho as the 39 **Captain of the Lord's Host** saying, *I have given Jericho into thine hand, and the king thereof, [and] the mighty men of valor.*[354] This marks the day when Jesus leaves the Holiest Place and changes His priestly garments for those of a warrior King. Israel marched around the city for seven days led by seven trumpets. And on the 7th day, Israel circled the city seven times and at the 40 **last Trump,** the 41 *walls came tumbling down.*[355]

Walls of Sin Fall: the Last Trump

Likewise, the walls of sin shall come tumbling down at the Last Trump. *In a moment, in the twinkling of an eye, at the last*

---

[347] Romans 2:29; Jeremiah 4:4.

[348] Joshua 5:10.

[349] Joshua 5:11.

[350] Joshua 5:12.

[351] This is yet apart of another helical wave transform!

[352] Joshua 6:1.

[353] Revelation 15:8.

[354] Joshua 5:13-15. Revelation 14:14; Revelation 19:11.

[355] Joshua 6:16, 20.

trump: for the trumpet shall sound, and the dead shall be raised incorruptible, and we shall be changed. For this corruptible must put on incorruption, and this mortal [must] put on immortality. So when this corruptible shall have put on incorruption, and this mortal shall have put on immortality, then shall be brought to pass the saying that is written, Death is swallowed up in victory.[356] I now understand that the falling of the 42 **great hail**[357] on the enemy will be the last plague that will usher the 43 **Second Coming of our Lord Jesus Christ just as the Sun Stood fast.**[358] And there was 44 a **very great slaughter, till they were consumed** pointing[359] to the slaughter of *the kings of the earth, and their armies, gathered together to make war against Him that sat on the horse, and against his army. And the beast was taken, and with him the false prophet that wrought miracles before him, with which he deceived them that had received the mark of the beast, and them that worshipped his image. These both were cast alive into a lake of fire burning with brimstone.* 45 And **in the end, God gave the land for an inheritance to all the tribes of Israel.**[360] Likewise, Jesus will give *an inheritance incorruptible, and undefiled, and that fadeth not away, reserved in heaven for you, Who are kept by the power of God through faith unto salvation ready to be revealed in the last time.*[361]

Some Guardians are deliberately presented back to back so that the events in the earthly and the heavenly walk of Jesus can be clearly communicated. These supernaturally connected pairs include David and Solomon and Moses and Joshua. We also see Elijah paired with Elisha as John the Baptist was paired with Jesus. This technique allows us to see the grand picture of the Plan of Salvation through the earthly walk of men.

---

[356] 1 Corinthians 15:52-54.
[357] Joshua 10:11; Revelation 16:21.
[358] Joshua 10:12, 13; Revelation 19:17. Genesis 19:22, 23.
[359] Joshua 10:20-27; Revelation 19:19-21.
[360] Joshua 11:23; 13:7; 18:10.
[361] 1 Peter 1:4, 5.

Testimony of Joshua Son of Nun

His name is "*Jehovah Saves*" the "*Son of Posterity*"
He leads the battle at the foot of the Mount and *wins as
the master's hands are held up*; *ASCENDS TO THE
MOUNT OF GOD; departs not from the Tabernacle.*
God does not forsake him or fail him all his days; And
he *meditates on the Book of the Law day and night.*
The ones that are spared bind the *scarlet cord* about
their opening of light (soul window).

The people of *ISRAEL MUST FOLLOW THE LORD* of
all the Earth by 2000 because Israel has not passed this
way before; The *Lord of all the Earth goes ahead by
2000* with the Ark and the waters are cut off; those
waters that back up *wash away sins all the way back
to Adam*; those waters that go down, empty sins into
the Dead Sea (**the wages of sin are death**) *PEOPLE
MUST PASS BEFORE THE ARK OF THE LORD;
REPROACH OF EGYPT IS ROLLED AWAY.*

The *CAPTAIN OF THE LORD'S HOST* appears and
fights the enemy for Israel. Tribulation trumpets
sound 7 days; circle the city 7 times (as if unfurling seals
of a scroll) on the 7th day. *GREAT SHOUT* at the *LAST
TRUMP* as the walls (of sin) fall; the *people ascend up*.

And the *LAST PLAGUE OF HAIL* comes and *THE SUN
STANDS STILL*. And stones are rolled over the pit at
the end of a great slaughter. And Israel is given a land
for which they did not labor, with cities and vineyards.
Choose Ye this Day Whom Ye Will Serve

In the next chapter, we explore the events in the lives of Moses and Joshua on the grand Stage we call the Sanctuary. The Sanctuary provides the dimension of space to the event sequence that we have been discovering. We see the Sanctuary Map superimposed on the geography of the Middle East. And upon this geographic stage we see the events of Moses and Joshua more clearly. But, more importantly, we see how the Divinely orchestrated movements on this stage point to the events in the Plan of Salvation. We discover that the events in the lives of Moses and Joshua align with the Sanctuary. And through this lens, we see clarification of the events found in the Revelation of John. We see the two witnesses, the sealing of Israel, the unfurling of the seven seals, and the seven trumpets. We see the last plague and the Last Trump. And we see the Second Coming and the time when the wicked are sealed in the pit. And finally, we see the destruction of the wicked followed by the inheritance given to the people of God.

11 *Divine Stage: Supernatural Cryptogram*

We have such an high priest, who is set on the right hand of the throne of the Majesty in the heavens; A minister of the sanctuary, and of the true tabernacle, which the Lord pitched, and not man... the example and shadow of heavenly things, as Moses was admonished of God for, See, saith he, [that] thou make all things according to the pattern showed to thee in the mount. Thy way, O God, [is] in the sanctuary: who [is so] great a God as [our] God?[362]

Upon the Mount, Moses was given the pattern[363] to make a replica of the Heavenly Sanctuary. It was a model constructed like a stage upon which actions taken on the earthly stage point to events taking place in their heavenly counterpart. Think about that! In every detail, the Sanctuary provides the framework of the Plan to Save mankind from sin. Every aspect of the Sanctuary from the objects, their locations, their colors, and their materials have prophetic significance. But the Sanctuary map is more than the Sanctuary transported by Israel in their journey in the Wilderness. It was also a map of their physical journey. More important than either of these, it provides the spiritual path by which all must travel to be saved. It is in Truth, the Way to Eternal Life.

---

[362] Hebrews 8:1-5; Psalm 77:13.
[363] Exodus 25 to 27.

The Sanctuary Stage

The Sanctuary is a map or cryptogram of the steps in the Plan of Salvation. Every step taken by the priests in the earthly Sanctuary, point to steps taken by Jesus in the heavenly Sanctuary. The Sanctuary and its features are the stage. The role of the priests in the daily sacrificial system and the annual feasts are a mirror of the steps that were taken by Jesus on Earth and are being taken by Jesus in heaven to free mankind from sin. The movements of the Plan are acted out by the priests. But most significantly, each step taken by Moses, Aaron, and Joshua from the bondage in Egypt to the Promised Land have blazed a time-sequence leading from Sin to Heaven. Even the geography of the Land was rolled out before them as a giant stage. In the beginning they walked onto the part of the stage we refer to as the camp outside the Court. Each step they took is like a Divine Play that prefigures Christ's very steps and they paved the way for all those that follow Jesus to heaven.

Thy Way is in the Sanctuary

The Sanctuary is an encrypted riddle of the mysterious and supernatural time sequence of events that Israel encountered along their journey from Egypt to the Promised Land. The Sanctuary is a spiritual map for every believer making their way out of the bondage of sin to the eternal bliss of the Promised Land. The miraculous connections between Jesus and Moses are outlined like a School Master through the objects and rituals of the Sanctuary. For it is said, *Thy way, O God, [is] in the sanctuary*...[364] Events surrounding the pattern of the earthly sanctuary unlock past, present, and even future events that are yet to unfold in the invisible realm of heaven. *The Sanctuary like the LAW were our schoolmasters [to bring us] unto Christ, that we might be justified by faith.*[365] *But after that faith is come, we are no longer under a schoolmaster. For ye are all the children of God by faith*

---

[364] Psalm 77:13.
[365] Galatians 3:23, 24.

in Christ Jesus. For as many of you as have been baptized into Christ have put on Christ. There is neither Jew nor Greek, there is neither bond nor free, there is neither male nor female: for ye are all one in Christ Jesus.[366] The events in the travels of Israel from Rameses (Tanis) in Egypt to Mount Nebo foreshadow the events of Jesus from the crucifixion to His work in the Holy Place of the Sanctuary. Joshua's walk shows how the events from the Jordan to the Promised Land trace the events in the ministry of Jesus from the Holy Place to the Holiest Place in the Sanctuary to His Second Coming and our Deliverance to the Promised Land.

I AM the Door

Israel [1] **was in bondage** in Egypt long before the birth of Moses, just as was the setting at the time of the birth of Jesus. Moses and his brother Aaron were sent repeatedly to warn the prideful Pharaoh to let the People of God go but the Pharaoh stubbornly resisted. And with each unheeded warning there was a more grievous plague. Each warning was an escalation over the one before. [2] Likewise, Jesus and the Holy Spirit **performed miracles encouraging the devil to let the people of Israel go**. In the end, the people of Israel were instructed to place the blood of the lamb over their [3] **door posts,**[367] **unaware that this "transform" pointed to Jesus who covers the posts of their minds and hearts with His saving blood.** *It also pointed to the Door to the Court.*[368] Jesus later said, *I AM the door: by me if any man enter in, he shall be saved, and shall go in and out,* [369] *and find pasture.* [4] The Lord said, **Israel [is] my son, [even] my firstborn...***if thou refuse to let him go, behold, I will slay thy son, [even] thy firstborn.*[370] [5] Satan working through Pharaoh and Herod, pridefully **miscalculated the power of God in the slaying of the first born**. Christ and Satan were bound in a deadly war.

---

[366] Galatians 3:25-28.
[367] Exodus 12:7.
[368] Numbers 3:26.
[369] John 10:9.
[370] Exodus 4:22; 23.

Brazen Altar: Passover Sacrifice

The ⑥ **lamb was to be slain on the 14ᵗʰ day** in the ⑦ **evening just as Jesus was slain on the ninth hour**[371] *of the 14ᵗʰ day known as the Passover*. Moreover, Israel was also ⑧ **instructed not to break a bone of the lamb**, which points to the death of Jesus. The Roman soldiers routinely broke the bones of those being crucified, but when they came to the body of Jesus, He was already dead. So instead they pierced His side. The people of Israel didn't know it then, but the Lord was painting a picture of the sacrifice of Jesus, the innocent, sinless Lamb of God, whose blood stained the posts of the Cross.

The Passover would later be celebrated in the Sanctuary. The Court of the Sanctuary represents the world **which spiritually is called Sodom and** ⑨ **Egypt, where also our Lord was crucified.**[372] ⑩ **The blood on the door posts, the Brazen Altar, and the Cross** are all meant to point us to **the Lamb of God, which taketh away the sins of the world.**[373] How could the people deny Jesus. The evidence was too conspicuous. And the Lord instructed Israel to take a ⑪ **lamb without blemish**[374] on the ⑫ **10ᵗʰ day of the first month,**[375] just as Jesus would be selected as the lamb without sin, over 1400 years later. Israel didn't realize that each step was a shadow of the future. ⑬ **The lamb was selected to protect Israel with its covering blood** just as those of Spiritual Israel are saved by the covering blood of Jesus. ⑭ **Both Pharaoh and Satan lost at the sacrifice of the First born** [376] for it was through the great sacrifice that Satan, the self-proclaimed God of Egypt, lost to the God of Israel.

---

[371] Matthew 27:46.
[372] Revelation 11:8.
[373] John 1:29.
[374] Exodus 12:5.
[375] Exodus 12:2, 3.
[376] Colossians 1:18; Hebrews 11:28.

Unleavened Bread: Bread of Life

On the 14th day and for the following 7 days, Israel was to eat unleavened bread. The Lord was again painting another picture of the death of Jesus. No leaven was to be eaten nor found in the house. I now know that ⌷15⌷ **leaven is a symbol of sin.**[377] And the people *baked unleavened cakes of the dough which they brought forth out of Egypt, for it was not leavened; because they were thrust out of Egypt, and could not tarry, neither had they prepared for themselves any victual.*[378] The ⌷16⌷ **body of Jesus was striped and pierced as was the unleavened bread.** Jesus, the bread of life, the One without sin, was to be represented as ⌷17⌷ **unleavened bread.** The people were enacting the death of Christ. Who, but God, could know these details in advance?

First Fruits: Jesus the Firstborn

Before Israel left Egypt, the Lord demanded that the First born of every household be consecrated to the Lord, even the households of Egypt. Moses was directed by the Lord to go to the Pharaoh and say, *Israel [is] my son, [even] my firstborn: And I say unto thee, Let my son go, that he may serve me: and if thou refuse to let him go, behold, I will slay thy son, [even] thy firstborn.*[379] I now realize that God promised to give Jesus, ⌷18⌷ **the First-born of heaven** to save sinners. Even after the miraculous plagues that God brought upon Egypt, the ⌷19⌷ **Pharaoh stubbornly refused because of selfish pride, a reflection of the pride of Satan.** As a consequence, the destroying angel was given the order to destroy the first born of both man and beast except for those that had the blood of the lamb of God on their door posts. After the judgment was brought upon Egypt, the Lord said, *Sanctify unto me all the firstborn, whatsoever openeth the womb among the children of*

---

[377] Leviticus 16:16, 17.
[378] Exodus 12:34, 39.
[379] Exodus 4:22, 23.

Israel, [both] of man and of beast: it [is] mine.[380] *And it came to pass, when Pharaoh would hardly let us go, that the LORD slew all the firstborn in the land of Egypt, both the firstborn of man, and the firstborn of beast: therefore I sacrifice to the LORD all that openeth the matrix, being males; but all the firstborn of my children I redeem.*[381] Jesus is the firstborn of Heaven and He was brought out of 20 **Egypt where He was slain in the figure.**[382] 21 **Jesus Christ, is the faithful witness, [and] the first begotten of the dead,** *and the prince of the kings of the earth. Unto him that loved us, and washed us from our sins in his own blood.*[383] 22 He is the firstborn of many brethren **Who is the image of the invisible God,** *the* 23 **Firstborn of every creature.**[384] Jesus is the 24 **First Fruit of Heaven.**[385] Needless to say, Pharaoh set the captives free!

Laver and Veil: Parting Red Sea

Soon after Israel arrived at the Red Sea, they were hopelessly trapped between the Red Sea and Pharaoh's army of chariots. The laver, referred to as the molten sea[386] 25 **points to the Red Sea as a symbol of cleansing**. The "red" in Red Sea also points to the cleansing blood of Jesus.[387] The laver was used by the priests to cleanse themselves after they sacrificed an animal at the Brazen Alter. The priests were to enter the Holy Place only after they had cleansed themselves. The purification of the priests in the Laver

---

[380] Exodus 13:1, 2 and 11-16; Numbers 3:13.

[381] Exodus 13:15. See also Deuteronomy Chapter 26.

[382] Hosea 11:1; Matthew 2:15; Revelation 11:8.

[383] Revelation 1:5.

[384] Colossians 1:15.

[385] Mark 16:9.

[386] Interestingly, the rim of the sea was ornamented with flowers like lilies and below the rim was a border of vines and gourds. The gourds themselves are symbols of death, burial, and resurrection since the word means *to break open to bring forth seed*. The seed is the Word, and the great commission is to spread the Word *baptizing them in the name of the Father, the Son, and the Holy Ghost*. (Matthew 28:19).

[387] 1 Corinthians 10:1-4.

also points to the baptism of Jesus, our High Priest. Likewise, according to Paul, the parting of the waters of the 26 **Red Sea represents the baptism of the people** and *the cloud represents the Holy Spirit that fills them*. As Paul would later write, *Moreover, brethren, I would not that ye should be ignorant, how that all our fathers were under the cloud, and all passed through the sea; And were all baptized unto Moses in the cloud and in the sea; And did all eat the same spiritual meat; And did all drink the same spiritual drink: for they drank of that spiritual Rock that followed them: and that Rock was Christ.*[388] I now realize that 27 **the opening of the Red Sea pointed to the opening of the Veil to the Holy Place**. Jesus led Israel step by step like a School Master[389] to point to events in His own walk that would free Spiritual Israel from sin.

Candlesticks: the Burning Bush

Moses said, *I kept the flock of Jethro* [my] *father in law, the priest of Midian: and* [I] *led the flock to the backside of the desert, and came to* the mountain of God, *[even] to Horeb. And the angel of the LORD appeared unto Moses in a flame of fire out of the midst of a bush: ... and, behold, the bush burned with fire, and the bush [was] not consumed...God called unto Moses out of the midst of the bush, and said, Moses, Moses. And Moses said, Here [am] I. And he said, Draw not nigh hither: put off thy shoes from off thy feet, for the place whereon thou standest [is]* holy ground.*[390]* 28 I now realize that **the vision that Moses had was of Jesus in the Holy Place. It is like unto the vision that John had of Jesus after His ascension**. It is written by John saying, *I saw seven golden candlesticks; And in the midst of the seven candlesticks [one] like unto the Son of man, clothed with a garment down to the foot, and girt about the paps with a golden girdle. His head and [his] hairs [were] white like wool, as white as snow; and his eyes [were] as a flame of fire; And his feet like*

---

[388] 1 Corinthians 10:1-4.
[389] Galatians 3:24, 25.
[390] Exodus 3:1-5.

unto fine brass, as if they burned in a furnace; and his voice as the sound of many waters.[391] The One John saw in the Holy Place of the sanctuary is the same Jesus that Moses saw in the Pillar Cloud, the same Jesus that Moses saw in the burning bush, the same Jesus that spoke to Moses face to face in the Sanctuary, and the same Jesus that spoke to the apostle John. *Then spake Jesus… saying,* 29 **the seven candlesticks which thou sawest are the seven churches.**[392] *I am the light of the world: he that followeth me shall not walk in darkness, but shall have the light of life.*[393] The burning bush points to Jesus among the candlesticks. He is the One that gives illumination to the Churches.

Table of Shewbread: Manna

After the Lord brought Israel across the Red Sea they *went out into the wilderness of Shur; and they went three days in the wilderness, and found no water.*[394] The Lord heard the prayers of Moses and they *came to Elim, where [were] twelve wells of water, and threescore and ten palm trees: and they encamped there by the waters.*[395] I now realize that after Jesus was baptized He surrounded himself with 30 **twelve apostles that are symbolized by the twelve wells** and by 31 **70 disciples symbolized by the 70 palm trees.** Likewise, 32 **out of the apostles and disciples flowed the living water of the Holy Spirit springing up into everlasting life.**[396] Again, Moses built an altar of 33 **12 pillars according to the 12 tribes, the pillars of Israel.**[397] And likewise, **Moses selected the 70 elders**[398] **to help guide the people.** And Israel journeyed from *Elim, and … came unto the wilderness of Sin, which [is] between Elim and Sinai, on the fifteenth day of the second month after their departing out of the land of Egypt.*

---

[391] Revelation 1:12-15.
[392] Revelation 1:20.
[393] John 8:12.
[394] Exodus 15:22.
[395] Exodus 15:27.
[396] John 4:14.
[397] Exodus 24:4; Numbers 1:44 and 17:6.
[398] Exodus 24:1, 9.

And the children of Israel said unto them, Would to God we had died by the hand of the LORD in the land of Egypt, when we sat by the flesh pots, [and] when we did eat bread to the full; for ye have brought us forth into this wilderness, to kill this whole assembly with hunger.[399] It is written, **Our fathers did eat manna in the desert; as it is written, He gave them bread from heaven to eat... 34 the Father gives us the true bread from heaven. For the bread of God is he which cometh down from heaven, and giveth life unto the world... I am the bread of life: 35 he that cometh to Me shall never hunger; and he that believeth on Me shall never thirst.[400]** The manna is represented by the Table of Shewbread and it in turn points forward to Jesus. After Israel left the Wilderness of Sin they camped in Rephidim where **the Lord brought forth water from the Rock[401]** which 37 **symbolizes the pierced side of Jesus, our Rock** that brought forth living water.[402] There Moses raised the rod with stretched out arms while Joshua defeated Amalek at the foot of the hill. *The stretched out arms of Moses upon the hill 38* **symbolized Jesus with His arms stretched out upon the Cross** on a hill called Golgotha. One hand was held by Hur, meaning Liberty and whiteness like that of the *Holy Spirit*. The other hand was held by Aaron, the *High Priest*. I now realize that the events in wilderness were used by the Lord as a School Master to teach about His Plan of Salvation. Even the supporting "actors" like Hur and Aaron have eternal significance in the Plan.

Altar of Incense: Mount Sinai

On the 1st day of the third month since leaving Egypt, Israel arrived in the wilderness of Mount Sinai and camped before the Mount. The very Mount where Moses had met Jesus in the Burning Bush. And on the third day the Lord came unto Israel in a thick cloud and smoke ascended from the Mount and there were

---

[399] Exodus 16:1-3.
[400] John 6:31-35; also John 6:47-51; and Exodus 16:1-36.
[401] Exodus 17:6.
[402] John 4:10, 11.

thunders and lightnings and the camp trembled and the Mount quaked. And the voice of the Lord sounded as a trumpet louder and louder and the Lord spoke unto Moses as with a voice. And Moses climbed the Mount and it was there that God gave Israel His Commandments at His altar.[403] Moses later wrote five books referred to as the Torah or the 39 **Law of Moses that points to the LAW of God and His Sanctuary Plan.** I now realize that **Mount Sinai** 40 **represents the fire of the Altar of Incense in the Sanctuary where the prayers of the people ascend to God**, mixed with incense. The fire and smoke that descended upon the Mount are also 41 **prophetic symbols of the flames of the Holy Spirit that descended upon those that remained in Jerusalem** on the very same day at the end of the Feast of Weeks known as 42 **Pentecost.**[404] God gave us the LAW on the day of Pentecost just as the Holy Spirit transformed the hearts of those waiting in Jerusalem for the Comforter. This fulfills the prophecy of Jeremiah as it is written, *Behold, the days come, saith the LORD, that I will make a new covenant with the house of Israel, and with the house of Judah: Not according to the covenant[405] that I made with their fathers in the day [that] I took them by the hand to bring them out of the land of Egypt; which my covenant they brake, although I was an husband unto them, saith the LORD: But this [shall be] the covenant that I will make with the house of Israel; After those days, saith the LORD, I will put my law in their inward parts, and write it in their hearts; and will be their God, and they shall be my people.*[406] The old Covenant established at Sinai is replaced by the birth of the newly redeemed people at Jerusalem[407] which is above. And in 42 those days the blood of the animal sacrifices will be done away with by **Jesus the mediator of the new covenant, and to the blood of sprinkling, that speaketh better things than [that of] Abel.**[408]

---

[403] Exodus Chapter 20.
[404] Acts 2:1-4. Leviticus 23:16.
[405] Exodus 24:8.
[406] Jeremiah 31:31-33.
[407] Hebrews 8:8, 13.
[408] Hebrews 12:24.

Parallel Steps of Moses and Christ

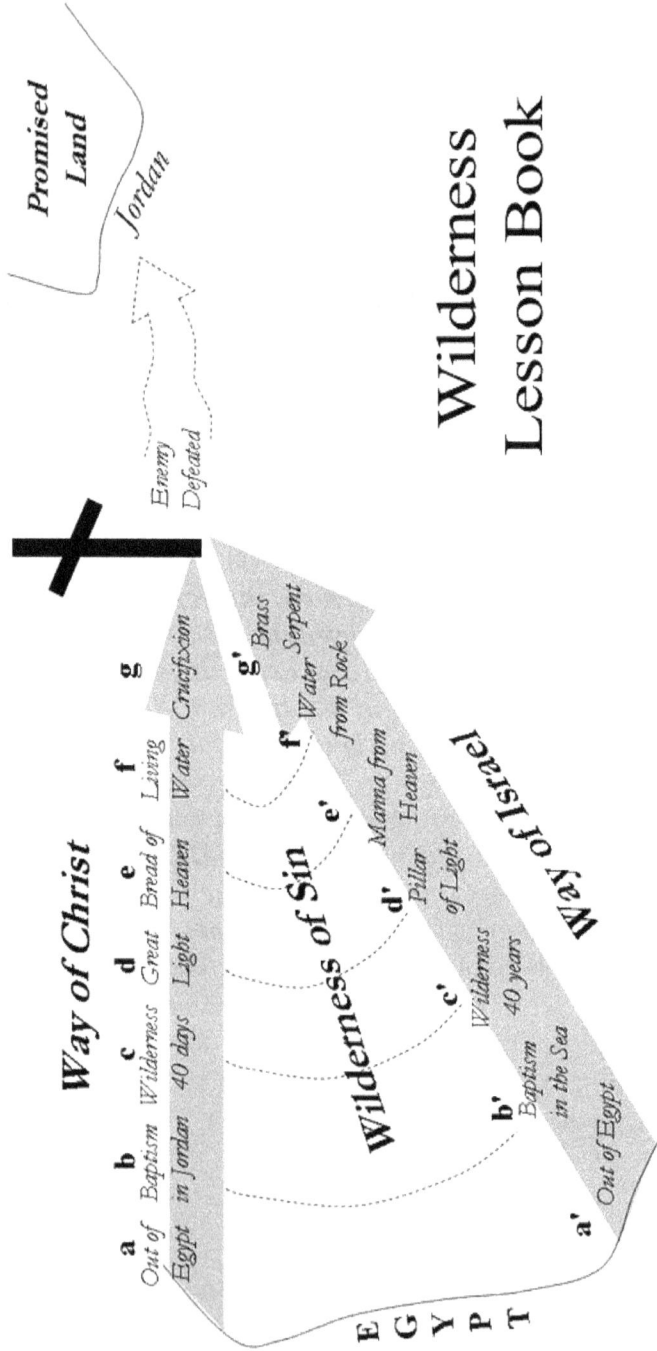

Wilderness
Lesson Book

Promised
Land

Jordan

Enemy
Defeated

Way of Christ

a — Out of Egypt
b — Baptism in Jordan
c — Wilderness 40 days
d — Great Light
e — Bread of Heaven
f — Living Water
g — Crucifixion

Wilderness of Sin

g' Brass Serpent
f' Water from Rock
e' Manna from Heaven
d' Pillar of Light
c' Wilderness 40 years
b' Baptism in the Sea
a' Out of Egypt

Way of Israel

E
G
Y
P
T

The Lord gave Israel the two Tablets of Stone whereupon He cut the Commandments with fire from His own hand.[409] Likewise, the fire of the 43 **Holy Spirit wrote the Commandments on the hearts of those that waited until the Pentecost in Jerusalem.**[410] And at the Mount 3000 perished which 44 **points to the 3000 that died of their old selves and were reborn at Jerusalem.**[411] 45 You could say that fire cut the Law on the tablets of stone just as Jesus writes the Law on the stony hearts of men. The LAW given at Sinai was a *law of carnal death* because no one could keep it perfectly, except Jesus. But the gift of Christ through His sacrifice and blood is the 46 *law of spiritual life* through GRACE.

Brazen Serpent: Cross of Jesus

After building the Sanctuary, Israel spent nearly 40 years in the wilderness learning numerous lessons. All the objects, practices, and events were given to us as *ensamples: and they are written for [your] admonition, upon whom the ends of the world are come.*[412] And Jesus said, *As Moses lifted up the serpent in the wilderness,* 47 *even so must the Son of man be lifted up: That whosoever believeth in him should not perish, but have eternal life. For God so loved the world, that he gave his only begotten Son, that whosoever believeth in him should not perish, but have everlasting life. For God sent not his Son into the world to condemn the world; but that the world through him might be saved.*[413] At the end of his life, Moses anointed Joshua and he ascended **Mount Nebo** to look over into the Promised Land just as Jesus would ascend the 48 **Mount of Olives to look over the beautiful City of Jerusalem**. And when Moses died at the age of 120 years, Joshua began his mission of leading the people of Israel into the glorious Canaan.

---

409 Exodus 24:12, 31:18; 34:1-4.
410 Acts 1:5; and Acts Chapter 2.
411 Exodus 32:28; Acts 2:41; Romans 5:20.
412 1 Corinthians 10:11.
413 John 3:14-17.

Jesus the Lamb of God
PASSOVER
Crucifixion (Mark 15:25; Romans 6:6; Galatians 2:20)

1 Lamb found without blemish (Ex 12:5; 1 Peter 1:19)
2 Lamb set aside 4 days on 10th of Nisan
3 Selected to bear sins when chosen
4 Lamb slain (Revelation 13:8)
5 Lamb killed between evenings at 3PM (Mark 15:34)
6 Lambs bones not broken (Psalm 34:20)

FEAST OF UNLEAVENED BREAD
Sabbath Rest in the Tomb (1 Corinthians 5:7)

7 Bread without sin (leaven); Jesus without sin
8 Body pierced and striped like unleavened bread

FIRST FRUITS
Resurrection and Ascension (John 20:17)

9   First born of the dead (Revelation 1:5)
10 First born of many brethren (Romans 8:29)
11 First born of every creature (Colossians 1:15)
12 Worthy Wave Sheaf Offering (Revelation 5:12)

PENTECOST
Gift of the Holy Spirit (Jeremiah 31:31-34)

13 Fire descends on Mount Sinai; Fire descends on the
    heads of the apostles and disciples (Acts 2:1-4)
14 Moses give Law on the day of Pentecost; Jesus sends the
    Holy Spirit on Pentecost (Leviticus 23:16; Acts 2:1)
15 Birth of Israel; Birth of newly redeemed Israel
16 3000 die; 3000 die of former self and are reborn
17 Fire cuts Commandments on stone (Ex. 24:13); fire cuts
    Commandments on their hearts (Acts 1:5; 2)

Transition: Moses to Joshua

The transition between Moses and Joshua is of greatest significance. 49 Simply put, **Moses represents the walk of Jesus upon the Earth.** 50 **Joshua represents the work of Jesus in Heaven.** 51 As the wanderings of Israel approached the **end of 40 years**, numerous events took place foreshadowing events at the end of **Christ's last 40 days on earth.** The end of the 40 years[414] came at a time when the Manna would stop falling from heaven. Just as at the end of Christ's 40 days, 52 Jesus the **Bread of Life was no longer with the people in Israel.** 53 Likewise, the end of the 40 years came at the time when the Pillar cloud would stop leading Israel on Earth. And just as the Pillar Cloud ceased, so also, **at the end of Christ's 40 days, the Light of the World was no longer with the world.**[415] 54 And **as Jesus turned over His work on Earth to the Comforter at His ascension; so Moses turned his work over to Joshua.**

But the transition from Moses to Joshua is far more than a foreshadowing of events during the last 40 days of Christ's life. 55 It is far more than Christ's figurative **crossing of the Jordan represented by His crossing from the Mount of Olives to heaven.** The transition in the passing of the work from Moses to Joshua points even further into the future when Christ's work transitions from the Holy Place of the Sanctuary to His entry into the Holiest Place. 56 **It points to the time when Jesus, as High Priest, would enter <u>into the Holiest Place ONCE to cleanse the sins of all of Israel.</u>** It points to the time when **Jesus would cross through the veil and stand before the Ark of the Covenant** where He stands today to wash away the sins of the world.[416]

Christ is not entered into the holy places made with hands, [which are] the figures of the true; 57 *but into heaven itself, now to appear in the presence of God for us: Nor yet that he*

---

[414] Numbers 14: 32-35.
[415] John 7:33.
[416] Hebrews 10:19-21; Acts 22:16; Isaiah 1:16; Galatians 1:4; 1 John 2:2.

should offer himself often, as the high priest entereth into the holy place every year with blood of others; For then must he often have suffered since the foundation of the world: ⑤⑧ **but now once in the end of the world hath he appeared to put away sin by the sacrifice of Himself.** *And as it is appointed unto men once to die, <u>but after this the judgment</u>...*[417]

Messengers: Angel's Messages

Israel overcame the serpents in the Wilderness of Sin, defeated their enemies, and took the Promised Land. ⑤⑨ **Likewise, the armies of Jesus will soon defeat Satan and his forces and set the captives free from sin and death.** And ⑥⓪ **just as the waters of the Jordan, <u>let judgment run down as waters,</u> <u>and righteousness as a mighty stream</u>,**[418] so will Israel be cleansed.

Nearly 38 years before the Crossing of the Jordan, Joshua was sent by Moses to spy on the land of Canaan. Joshua was in awe and marveled at the towering great walled cities. Joshua had ⑥① the **Faith of Jesus**[419] because He watched as the Angel of the Lord brought Israel out of Egypt and parted the Red Sea. Jesus was the Angel that went before Israel in the Pillar Cloud and guided Israel to the land Promised to Abraham.[420] But those that searched the land of Canaan with Joshua didn't have faith that Israel would overcome. Because of their unbelief[421] God sent Israel back into the wilderness for 40 years to build the faith of the people. When it was time for Israel to cross the Jordan after 40 years of schooling in the wilderness, like Moses before him, Joshua sent two messengers[422] to search out the land across Jordan. The two messengers were sent to search out the land and measure the people[423] just as ⑥② **two angels**[424] were sent into Sodom before its

---

[417] Hebrews 9:24-27.
[418] Amos 5:24.
[419] Galatians 3:22-26.
[420] Numbers 14:6-14:9.
[421] Matthew 13:58.
[422] Joshua 6:25.
[423] Revelation 11:1.

destruction. The **two messengers, sent to Jericho,** came to the place of Rahab, a harlot, and she gave them shelter because she was convinced that the God of Israel would prevail. *And she said unto the men, I know that the LORD hath given you the land, and that your terror is fallen upon us, and that all the inhabitants of the land faint because of you. For we have heard how the LORD dried up the water of the Red sea for you, when ye came out of Egypt; and what ye did unto the two kings of the Amorites, that [were] on the other side Jordan, Sihon and Og, whom ye utterly destroyed. And as soon as we had heard [these things], our hearts did melt, neither did there remain any more courage in any man, because of you: for the LORD your God, he [is] God in heaven above, and in earth beneath.*[425]

The Lord is sending two messengers into the world today, [63] just like the two messengers that Joshua sent to Jericho, to warn the world of the end time Judgment. John the Revelator spoke of the **two Witnesses**[426] that prophecy for a thousand two hundred and three score days. [64] These *two Witnesses* spoken of by John are **the Old and New Testaments** and their messages are being carried by angel messengers, even the churches,[427] to warn the people of the impending judgement of mankind, *saying with a loud voice, Fear God, and give glory to him; for the hour of his judgment is come: and worship him that made heaven, and earth, and the sea, and the fountains of waters.*[428] *All nations have drunk of the wine of the wrath of her fornication, and the kings of the earth have committed fornication with her...Come out of her, my people, that ye be not partakers of her sins, and that ye receive not of her plagues.*[429] I now realize that [65] **harlots like Rahab** represent the spiritual daughters[430] of the evil systems brought by Satan to deceive and corrupt the whole world. God is

---

[424] Genesis 19:1.
[425] Joshua 2:9-11.
[426] Revelation 11:3.
[427] Revelation 1:20.
[428] Revelation 14:7.
[429] Revelation 18:3, 4.
[430] Revelation 17:5.

calling the world to come out of these false, corrupt, and evil systems before it is too late.

Rahab heard the message of the two witnesses and it was by faith in the God of the Hebrews that Rahab was saved |66| just as in the last days men will be saved **which keep the commandments of God, and have the testimony of Jesus Christ.**[431] True faith brings forth actions that verify faith. |67| **Rahab's faith produced the greatest work;**[432] giving testimony and bringing her family into the house marked by the Lord that they might be saved. And **like the blood over the door posts of Egypt, Rahab hung the red cord from her window.** These both are |68| **symbols of the blood that Jesus shed to save the world.** It is this same **red thread that runs through the Scriptures.** Rahab's faith in the God of Abraham saved herself and her family from death. Like Rahab, Gentiles and Jews alike are saved by the grace of Jesus. God works in strange and mysterious ways for in the end, Rahab became the great-grandmother of King David. |69| **The red cord that connected Rahab to Jesus represents the blood line of the Seed.** It is the **spiritual umbilical cord that binds us to Jesus**.

Veil to Holiest: Parting Jordan

|70| **The Jordan also is a figure that transforms the passage of Jesus our High Priest into the Holiest Place on the antitypical Day of Atonement**[433] to cleanse Israel and judge the living and the dead. Before Israel's passage, Joshua instructed the people of Israel saying, *Sanctify yourselves: for tomorrow the LORD will do wonders among you* just as the people had sanctified themselves in the wilderness in preparation for the **Day of Atonement.** And in the Jordan, as it is written, *judgment* did *run down as waters, and righteousness as a mighty stream.*[434]

---

[431] Revelation 12:17.
[432] Matthew 28:18-20.
[433] Leviticus 23:27-32.
[434] Amos 5:24.

After the two witnesses returned from the Mount,[435] the Lord of the whole Earth,[436] passed over the Jordan about 2000 before the people of Israel because the people had not passed this way before.[437] That is to say, *Jesus had preceded the people into heaven **about 2000** before the Spiritual Israel will cross over the* [71] *metaphorical Jordan*.

Jesus crosses the Heavenly veil to the Holiest Place as [72] **our High Priest to judge the living and the dead of Israel prior to His Second Coming.**[438]

John saw the antitypical Day of Atonement in vision saying, *the temple of God was opened in heaven, and there was seen in his temple the ark of his testament: and there were lightnings, and voices, and thunderings, and an earthquake, and great hail.*[439] For the time had come for *the dead, that they should be judged, and that thou shouldest give reward unto thy servants the*

---

[435] Joshua 2:23.
[436] Joshua 3:11.
[437] Joshua 3:4.
[438] Revelation 1:5-7.
[439] Revelation 11:19.

prophets, and to the saints, and them that fear thy name, small and great; and shouldest destroy them which destroy the earth.[440] Judgment would begin with Adam and the dead before the living.

Cross before the Ark in Judgment

It came to pass, when the people removed from their tents, to pass over Jordan, and the priests bearing the ark of the covenant before the people; And as they that bare the ark were come unto Jordan, and the feet of the priests that bare the ark were dipped in the brim of the water, (for Jordan overfloweth all his banks all the time of harvest,) That the waters which came down from above stood [and] rose up upon an heap very far from the city <u>*Adam*</u>*, that [is] beside Zaretan: and those that came down toward the sea of the plain, [even] the salt sea, failed, [and] were cut off: and the people passed over right against Jericho.*[441] Each person of the tribe of Israel passed in front of the Ark of the Covenant $\boxed{73}$ **just as the people in the last days are crossing in front of the Ark of the Covenant in heaven.** All the sins of the people are carried away in the heavenly sanctuary just as the waters of the Jordan *stood [and] rose up upon an heap* all the way back to **Adam**[442] and the waters were carried to the Dead Sea. How appropriate that the $\boxed{74}$ **judgment began with Adam,** because *judgment must begin at the house of God.*[443] *And the priests that bare the ark of the covenant of the LORD stood firm on dry ground in the midst of Jordan, and all the Israelites passed over on dry ground, until all the people were* <u>*passed clean*</u> *over Jordan.*[444] And how appropriate that our sins are carried to the **Dead Sea** $\boxed{75}$ for **the wages of sin is death but the gift of God [is] eternal life through Jesus Christ our Lord.**[445]

---

[440] Revelation 11:18.
[441] Joshua 3:14-16.
[442] Joshua 3:16.
[443] 1 Peter 4:17.
[444] Joshua 3:17.
[445] Romans 6:23.

24 Stones: 12 Saved and 12 Lost

Twelve representatives, one from each tribe, were appointed to *pass over before the ark of the LORD … into the midst of Jordan, and take …up every man … a stone upon his shoulder, according unto the number of the tribes of the children of Israel:… and these stones shall be for a memorial unto the children of Israel forever.*[446] The ⎡76⎤ **twelve stones on the west bank of the Jordan represent the redeemed of the Lord that are saved in the judgment.** All those that passed before the ark of the covenant and were washed clean of their sins and sealed. These are they that keep the commandments of God and have the faith of Jesus. And likewise, Joshua, a ⎡77⎤ figure of Jesus *set up twelve stones in the midst of Jordan, in the place where the feet of the priests which bare the ark of the covenant stood: and they are there unto this day.*[447] *The twelve stones left in the midst of the Jordan symbolize those that refuse to accept Jesus as their Savior.* ⎡78⎤ **They are weighed in the balances, and art found wanting.**[448] Like the Egyptian soldiers that scoffed at the God of Israel and were drowned in the Red Sea and like those in the days of Noah that scoffed and refused to board the sanctuary refuge that God provided them in Noah's Ark, ⎡79⎤ **the twelve stones left behind in the waters of the Jordan are symbols of the graves of those that choose to reject God.** ⎡80⎤ **The Jordan is a symbol of the death, burial, and resurrection of Jesus**. Those that choose Him will be resurrected. Those that refuse Him will be left behind.

Probation Closes: Jordan Closes

As soon as the feet of the priests carrying the Ark of the Covenant stepped into the edge of the Jordan, its waters were opened. ⎡81⎤ **The Ark was carried into the midst of the Jordan signaling the beginning of the judgment; the exiting of the ark from the**

---

[446] Joshua 4:5-7.
[447] Joshua 4.9.
[448] Daniel 5:7; Ecclesiastes 1:15.

Jordan signals the close of judgment.[449] *And it came to pass, when the priests that bare the ark of the covenant of the LORD were come up out of the midst of Jordan, [and] the soles of the priests' feet were lifted up unto the dry land, that the waters of Jordan returned unto their place, and flowed over all his banks, as [they did] before.*[450] **82** With the return of the river to its banks, **the passageway across the Jordan was closed, just as the veil to the temple in heaven will be closed.** John wrote of the future, saying *the temple was filled with smoke from the glory of God, and from his power; and no man was able to enter into the temple, till the seven plagues of the seven angels were fulfilled.*[451] The warnings had been given. The judgment of the quick and the dead was complete and the veil was closed. **83** **Just as the finger of God wrote on the Walls of Babylon, the fate of all men will be decided.** For the lost, like those in Babylon in the days of Daniel, many *art weighed in the balances, and art found wanting.*[452] **84** **When the books in heaven are closed, the people will be separated into two groups: those to be resurrected at Christ's return and those that will be lost.** The lost, represented by the monument of the twelve stones in the Jordan will be left behind and eroded away from memory. **85** **When the judgment is finished, the heavenly Court will be closed and none will be able to enter.** As Israel crossed into the Promised land, *Jericho was straitly shut up because of the children of Israel: none went out, and none came in.*[453] And in the words of Isaiah the prophet, *the city of confusion is broken down: every house is shut up, that no man may come in. [There is] a crying for wine in the streets; all joy is darkened, the mirth of the land is gone.*[454] God had once said to Noah, *Come thou and all thy house into the ark; for thee have I seen righteous before me in this generation.*[455] Likewise, all those that are faithful will be saved before the Ark of the

---

[449] Hebrews 4:14-16; 10:19-22; 9:11-28; 8:1-5.
[450] Joshua 4:10, 11, and 18.
[451] Revelation 15:8.
[452] Daniel 5:26, 27.
[453] Joshua 6:1.
[454] Isaiah 24:10, 11.
[455] Genesis 7:1; 7:16, 18.

Covenant. 86 **But when the door to the Ark is closed, as it was in the days of Noah, probation will be closed.** And Jesus said, *as it was in the days of Noe, so shall it be also in the days of the Son of man. They did eat, they drank, they married wives, they were given in marriage, until the day that Noe entered into the ark, and the flood came, and destroyed them all.*[456]

Passover: Sealing the People

The Passover at Gilgal marked a new beginning for Israel. The cycle that Moses spoke of in Egypt marked the beginning of a new cycle in the Promised Land. 87 **It was here that the manna stopped and the people ate of the fruit of the land.**[457] The fruit of the land was left behind by those whose hearts melted with fear and fled at the sight of the oncoming army of Israel.[458] Can you imagine their terror as they watched the Lord of Israel open the waters of the Jordan? 88 **Forty years had elapsed since Israel celebrated the first Passover and Feast of Unleavened Bread in Egypt** as the Lord's appointed time.

After crossing the Jordan, Joshua led Israel to the camp before Gilgal. 89 **Gilgal means Golgotha in the Syriac language** and that is fitting because the blood of foreskins was spilled at Gilgal just as the blood of Jesus had been spilled at the foot of the Cross. 90 The Lord said, **This day have I rolled away the reproach of Egypt. Wherefore, the name of the place is called Gilgal unto this day.**[459] Jesus was sealed in the tomb on the Sabbath.[460] And the Seal of the Tomb was *rolled away just as the name Gilgal also means rolled away*! 91 And **just as blood was used to cover the doorposts on that fateful night in Egypt, so was the blood of the foreskins a symbol of the circumcision of the heart.** For *he [is] a Jew, which is one inwardly; and circumcision [is that] of the*

---

[456] Luke 17:26, 27.
[457] Joshua 5:11, 12.
[458] Joshua 5:1.
[459] Joshua 5:9.
[460] Matthew 27:66.

heart, in the spirit, [and] not in the letter; whose praise [is] not of men, but of God. [92] **The circumcision at Gilgal points to the sealing of the people at the end of time.**[461] *It was the sign of circumcision, a seal of the righteousness of the faith which [Abraham] being uncircumcised: that he might be the father of all them that believe, though they be not circumcised; that righteousness might be imputed unto them also.*[462] *The foundation of God standeth sure, having this seal, The Lord knoweth them that are his. And, Let everyone that nameth the name of Christ depart from iniquity.*[463] *And the LORD thy God will circumcise thine heart, and the heart of thy seed, to love the LORD thy God with all thine heart, and with all thy soul, that thou mayest live.*[464]

Captain of the Lord's Host: Jesus

It was before Jericho that [93] **Joshua stood on Holy Ground in the presence of the Angel of the Lord just as Moses had stood on Holy Ground before Him at the Burning Bush near Mount Sinai.** And it was before Jericho that Jesus, the **Captain of the Lord's host** revealed Himself to Joshua.

When Joshua went forth in the morning before the taking of Jericho, there appeared before him a warrior fully equipped for battle. And Joshua asked, *Art thou for us, or for our adversaries? and He said, As Captain of the host of the Lord am I now come.*[465] And the Lord said to Joshua, *See, I have given into thine hand Jericho, and the king thereof, [and] the mighty men of valour.*[466] [94] **The very Angel that spoke to Joshua that night was Jesus, King of Kings. Jesus the High Priest had changed His robes and would fight the battle for Israel.** He stood with sword in hand; the very same two edged sword that John saw. [95] **I**

---

[461] Romans 2:29.
[462] Romans 4:11.
[463] 2 Timothy 2:19.
[464] Deuteronomy 30:6.
[465] Joshua 5:13-15.
[466] Joshua 6:2.

now realize that the sword that He held is the WORD of God. *For the word of God [is] quick, and powerful, and sharper than any twoedged sword, piercing even to the dividing asunder of soul and spirit, and of the joints and marrow, and [is] a discerner of the thoughts and intents of the heart.*[467] And He gave orders saying, *ye shall compass the city, all [ye] men of war, [and] go round about the city once. Thus shalt thou do six days. And seven priests shall bear before the ark seven trumpets of rams' horns: and the seventh day ye shall compass the city seven times, and the priests shall blow with the trumpets. And it shall come to pass, that when they make a long [blast] with the ram's horn, [and] when ye hear the sound of the trumpet, all the people shall shout with a great shout; and the wall of the city shall fall down flat, and the people shall ascend up every man straight before him.*[468] This would not be a battle among men alone. **The battle is the Lord's.**[469] The directions that Jesus gave Joshua were exceedingly unusual.

96 **Our very steps parallel a supernatural battle.** Had Jesus allowed Joshua to look upon the supernatural world around him, he would have seen the plains, *full of horses and chariots round about* Jericho just as they were round about Elisha.[470] *For we wrestle not against flesh and blood, but against principalities, against powers, against the rulers of the darkness of this world, against spiritual wickedness in high [places].*[471] 97 **It was a battle between the forces of Christ and Satan that stood as a figure of the final battle before the Second Coming of Jesus.** We need the Lord and His agencies to guide us through our supernatural battles, just as He guided the victory at Jericho. *The LORD saveth not with sword and spear: for the battle [is] the LORD's.*[472] Jesus will soon finish His work before the Ark of the Covenant in His celestial Court. 98 **Then He will change his**

---

[467] Hebrews 4:12.
[468] Joshua 6:3-5.
[469] 2 Chronicles 20:15.
[470] 2 Kings 6:17.
[471] Ephesians 6:12.
[472] 1 Samuel 17:47.

**garments and come to the world as the King of Kings and Lord
of Lords**[473] but not until every attempt is made to save each and
every last soul. For *the Lord is not slack concerning his promise,
as some men count slackness; but is longsuffering to us-ward,
not willing that any should perish, but that all should come to
repentance.*[474]

Unfurling the Seals

The Lord uses the hosts of Israel as if they were following the
choreography of a Divine Play. And all the steps of Israel were
pointing to steps being taken by Jesus in the heavenly Sanctuary.
*For all these things happened unto [Israel] for ensamples: and
they are written for our admonition, upon whom the ends of the
world are come.*[475] Sealing began first at the house of Israel[476] and
next it would go to the house of the Gentiles.[477] 99 **Like the seals
of a powerful King's scroll, the City of Jericho was sealed and
none could enter and none could leave.**[478] 100 **So was the scroll
spoken of by John in vision. It had seven seals; 7 meaning
completeness or perfection.** It was so completely sealed that no
one in the entire Universe was Worthy to open this King's Scroll
for it was the Scroll maintained in the celestial Court by the Father
God of the entire Universe. As John has written, and many of
those including the 24 elders have witnessed, this scroll was held
by *the right hand of him that sat on the throne a book written
within and on the backside, sealed with seven seals. And I saw a
strong angel proclaiming with a loud voice, Who is worthy to
open the book, and to loose the seals thereof? And no man in
heaven, nor in earth, neither under the earth, was able to open
the book, neither to look thereon. And I wept much, because no
man was found worthy to open and to read the book, neither to
look thereon. And one of the elders saith unto me, Weep not:*

---

[473] 1 Timothy 6:15; Revelation 17:14; and Revelation 19:16.
[474] 2 Peter 3:9.
[475] 1 Corinthians 10:11.
[476] Matthew 10:5, 6.
[477] Acts 9:15.
[478] Joshua 6:1.

behold, the Lion of the tribe of Juda, the Root of David, hath prevailed to open the book, and to loose the seven seals thereof. And I beheld, and, lo, in the midst of the throne and of the four beasts, and in the midst of the elders, stood a Lamb as it had been slain, having seven horns and seven eyes, which are the seven Spirits of God sent forth into all the earth. And he came and took the book out of the right hand of him that sat upon the throne. And when he had taken the book, the four beasts and four [and] twenty elders fell down before the Lamb, having every one of them harps, and golden vials full of odours, which are the prayers of saints.[479]

The seven seals of John were warnings of judgment upon the Gentiles as enacted at Jericho. And only Jesus could open the seals of the Scroll in John's Revelation. And it was Jesus that unfurls the seals of the figurative City, itself a symbol of the world and its history. |101| **Each trip around Jericho symbolized the unfurling of a single seal which was especially relevant for a period of Earth's history.** Each revolution about Jericho symbolizes the warnings given to the world by the messengers of the church throughout the ages. The first seal was unlocked by Jesus, the apostles, and the early church.[480] The third seal presented a pair of balances[481] signifying the judgment for the days long after the works of the apostles. When the fifth seal was loosed we hear voices *saying, How long, O Lord, holy and true, dost thou not judge and avenge our blood on them that dwell on the earth?[482]* The time of the fifth seal marks the time of the martyrs[483] like Wycliffe, Jerome, and Huss who suffered like Jesus at the hands of those being influenced by Satan. And events in the heavens mark the timing of the sixth seal in Earth's history with a great earthquake, the sun blackened, the moon as blood, and the stars of heaven falling to the earth *as a fig tree casteth her*

---

[479] Revelation 5:1-8.
[480] Revelation 6:2.
[481] Revelation 6:5.
[482] Revelation 6:10.
[483] Fox's Book of Martyrs Or a History of the Lives, Sufferings, and Triumphant Deaths of the Primitive Protestant Martyrs. John Foxe. EBook #22400, English. ISO-8859-1.

untimely figs, when she is shaken of a mighty wind.[484] And then John *saw another angel ascending from the east, having the seal of the living God: and he cried with a loud voice to the four angels, to whom it was given to hurt the earth and the sea, Saying, Hurt not the earth, neither the sea, nor the trees, till we have sealed the servants of our God in their foreheads.*[485] Then will the coming of Jesus be near. And if you study history, you will learn that most of these signs are already recorded in the past!

Jericho's 7 Trumpets: Jubilee

And when the angel had opened the seventh seal, there was silence in heaven about the space of half an hour. And I saw the seven angels which stood before God; and to them were given <u>*seven trumpets*</u>.[486] *And another angel came and stood at the altar, having a golden censer; and there was given unto him much incense, that he should offer [it] with the prayers of all saints upon the golden altar which was before the throne. And the smoke of the incense, [which came] with the prayers of the saints, ascended up before God out of the angel's hand. And the angel took the censer, and filled it with fire of the altar, and cast [it] into the earth: and there were voices, and thunderings, and lightnings, and an earthquake. And the seven angels which had the seven trumpets prepared themselves to sound.*[487]

When Jesus leaves the Holiest Place with the golden censer, the seven trumpets sound the warning of His soon return. 102 **Still, Jesus is not willing that any should perish, but that all should come to repentance**.[488] Jesus is trying to get the attention of the lost before it is too late. And He commands the angels that *they should not hurt the grass of the earth, neither any green thing, neither any tree; but only those men which have not the seal of God in their foreheads.* Jesus is sending warnings to awaken the

---

[484] Revelation 6:12, 13.
[485] Revelation 7:2, 3.
[486] Revelation 8:1, 2.
[487] Revelation 8:3-6.
[488] 2 Peter 3:9.

world of the lost. Those without the cord of Jesus are in danger of being lost forever. And Satan is doing everything in his power to keep people from turning to Christ. *But if our gospel be hid, it is hid to them that are lost: In whom the god of this world hath blinded the minds of them which believe not, lest the light of the glorious gospel of Christ, who is the image of God, should shine unto them.*[489] And Satan is the god of this world.

Seventh Trump: Walls of Sin Fall

While Jesus continues His work before the Ark of the Covenant in the Holiest Place everyone must pass before the Ark. As Israel circled Jericho, all of the people in the City of Jericho came before the Ark of the Covenant. With each revolution of the Ark, the seals were unwound, **sounding their warnings age to age**. In the end of time, warnings will be sounded from the Celestial Throne throughout the entire earth, so that the lost will hear and turn to God before it is too late. Again, God choreographed Israel's march around Jericho to point to the events at the end of time. 103 On the last day of the opening of the 7th Seal **the seven angels which had the seven trumpets prepared themselves to sound.**[490] As Israel marched around the city seven times on that 7th day, led by the 7 Trumpets, trumpet after trumpet sounded pointing to events at the very end of time. 104 **Signs from heaven are poured out one after another with a sense of greatest urgency**. Trumpet warnings after trumpet warnings are given to awaken the souls of men. Like the sound of the trumpet in warfare, so shall these last day warnings ring loud that all will hear. **Those who turn and listen and grab hold of the red cord will be saved. But those that turn away and refuse Him will be lost forever.**

In the days of the voice of the seventh angel, when he shall begin to sound, the mystery of God should be finished, as he hath

---

[489] 2 Corinthians 4:3, 4.
[490] Revelation 8:6.

declared to his servants the prophets.[491] I now realize that the sounding of the seventh trumpet is an entire period of Earth's history at the end of time. But during that time, few will turn to Jesus at the sound of the trumpet warnings. |105| **To the saved, like Rahab and her family, the sounding of the trumpets are the joyous sounds of Jesus approaching to rescue His people.**

As Israel marched around Jericho, its great walls towered above them. To men, the walls of Jericho appeared impregnable. But to God they marked the feeble works of Satan. |106| **Each block in the fortress represents sin that separates God from His people.** But to God, these walls of sin must be taken down so that He may again be reunited with His people. *For I am persuaded, that neither death, nor life, nor angels, nor principalities, nor powers, nor things present, nor things to come, nor height, nor depth, nor any other creature, shall be able to separate us from the love of God, which is in Christ Jesus our Lord.*[492] The walls of Jericho represent our sins that Jesus is removing before the Ark of the Covenant by the cleansing power of His blood. What a play!

The Sounding of the Last Trump

|107| **And on that last hour as Israel circled the city with trumpets blaring, they stopped.** *And it came to pass at the seventh time, when the priests blew with the trumpets, Joshua said unto the people, Shout; for the LORD hath given you the city. So the people shouted when [the priests] blew with the trumpets: and it came to pass, when the people heard the sound of the trumpet, and the people shouted with a great shout, that the wall fell down flat, so that the people went up into the city, every man straight before him, and they took the city.*[493] And I now realize, that it was *by faith [that] the walls of Jericho fell down, after they were compassed about seven days.*[494] It was

---

[491] Revelation 10:7; Jeremiah 35:14-17.
[492] Romans 8:38, 39.
[493] Joshua 6:16, 20.
[494] Hebrews 11:30.

Jesus that removed the walls block by block. So will it be by faith, that the sins of the people will be rolled away. The angel continues to call God's people with the voice of a trumpet[495] saying, *Come out of her, my people, that ye be not partakers of her sins, and that ye receive not of her plagues.* Why do the people continue to live in the walled cities of sin? Why do their walls separate them from Jesus? *Multitudes, multitudes in the valley of decision: for the day of the LORD [is] near in the valley of decision.*[496] All they need to do is turn away from the wickedness of the world and grab onto the red cord of salvation. Our Jesus is standing in the heavenly Court today as our High Priest. **He has a far better city**[497] 108 **waiting for His people in the antitypical Jubilee**[498] **when the slaves will be freed from the sins of the world**.

Armageddon: Supernatural War

As Israel camped before the Jordan prior to their crossing, the kings of the world were frightened that their kingdoms would be lost. Their *hearts did melt, neither did there remain any more courage in any man, because of you: for the LORD your God, He [is] God in heaven above, and in earth beneath.*[499] The kings of the surrounding nations watched with trepidation to see how the citadel of Jericho would withstand the vast forces that camped across Jordan. 109 **So did the forces of Satan tremble as they saw the angelic hosts of Jesus marshal on the shores of Jordan.** The battle at Jericho was not only a war of the flesh. 110 **It symbolizes the spiritual warfare that is fought with the two-edged sword that represents the Word of God.** *For we wrestle not against flesh and blood, but against principalities, against powers, against the rulers of the darkness of this world, against spiritual wickedness in high [places]. Wherefore take unto you the whole armour of God, that ye may be able to withstand in the*

---

495 Revelation 8:13.
496 Joel 3:14.
497 Hebrews 11:10, 16; Revelation 21:1-27.
498 Leviticus 25:9-15, 54, 55.
499 Joshua 2:11.

evil day, and having done all, to stand.[500] Jericho was the first fruits of the land given by God's supernatural intervention.

In the time of the end they will be 111 **gathered… together into a place called in the Hebrew tongue Armageddon.**[501] Likewise, the kings that opposed Israel after Jericho was conquered, *__gathered themselves together__, and went up, they and all their hosts, and encamped before Gibeon, and made war against it.*[502] But the Lord said, *Fear them not: for I have delivered them into thine hand; there shall not a man of them stand before thee.* Like at Jericho, the battle is the Lord's. In those days, Israel conquered 31 kings and their armies. 112 Among these was the **king of Megiddo,** [503] the symbol of the place where the last great spiritual battle will be fought at a place called Armageddon. The word Armageddon is transliterated to Greek from Hebrew **har,** הר מגידו, (Strong H2022) meaning "a mountain" (as in a spiritual mountain) and *Megiddo* (Strong מְגִדּוֹ H4023) /meg-id-do'/ Megiddo, "a place of crowds," as the multitudes in the valley of decision.

When Jesus is completing His work in the Holiest Place He reviews the case of every person that passes before the Ark of the Covenant. For those that turn to Him, He cleanses them with His blood and seals them. But for those that stubbornly rejected Him there is nothing that He can do, for He gives them all the freedom to choose who they will follow. After He reviews the very last case, 113 **He leaves the Holiest Place with the sins of the people, just as the High Priest does on the end of the Day of Atonement.** 114 **As Israel travelled in the wilderness, the High Priest would then transfer these sins to the head of the scapegoat.**[504] Likewise, Jesus, our High Priest will cleanse the Sanctuary of sins and transfer them onto Satan, the scapegoat, and his forces of fallen demons. *Who shall not fear thee, O Lord, and*

---

[500] Ephesians 6:11, 12.
[501] Revelation 16:16.
[502] Joshua 10:5.
[503] Joshua 12:21.
[504] Leviticus 16:21, 22.

glorify thy name? for [thou] only [art] holy: for all nations shall come and worship before thee; for thy judgments are made manifest.[505] In the writings of John we learn what happens next. *The temple of the tabernacle of the testimony in heaven was opened: And the seven angels came out of the temple, having the seven plagues, clothed in pure and white linen, and having their breasts girded with golden girdles. And the temple was filled with smoke from the glory of God, and from his power; and no man was able to enter into the temple, till the seven plagues of the seven angels were fulfilled.*[506]

Hailstones Fall: Last Plague

After the Lord had given Jericho into Israel's hand, the kings of the surrounding countries plotted against them and they gathered together to make war against Israel. But the Lord said to Joshua, *Fear them not: for I have delivered them into thine hand; there shall not a man of them stand before thee.*[507] And *the LORD cast down great stones from heaven upon them unto Azekah, and they died: [they were] more which died with hailstones than [they] whom the children of Israel slew with the sword.*[508] 115 **I now realize that these hailstones point to the plague that is poured out of the vial by the seventh angel.** As it is written by John, *the seventh angel poured out his vial into the air; and there came a great voice out of the temple of heaven, from the throne, saying, It is done. And there fell upon men a great hail out of heaven, [every stone] about the weight of a talent: and men blasphemed God because of the plague of the hail; for the plague thereof was exceeding great.*[509]

As Jesus washes away the sins of humanity since Adam, the sins are collected in 7 vials or bowls. The 116 **seven vials poured out upon the earth are the sins that have been washed away from**

---

[505] Revelation 15:4.
[506] Revelation 15:5-8.
[507] Joshua 10:8.
[508] Joshua 10:11.
[509] Revelation 16:17, 21.

those that have been saved by the precious blood of Jesus. And these very same sins will be poured back upon the head of Satan and his demons as symbolized by the transfer of sins to the head of the scapegoat.[510] 117 **And these very sins that have traumatized humanity since Adam will destroy Satan and his demonic forces** as if they are burned in a lake of fire together with death and the grave.[511] They will die of the sins that they have poured on others throughout Earth's history. Satan and his demons lost at the Cross when the tables were turned. It was at the Cross that Jesus said, *All power is given unto me in heaven and in earth.*[512] And Joshua found five kings hid in a cave at Makkedah and ordered his men to *roll great stones upon the mouth of the cave, and set men by it for to keep them.*[513] 118 **This points to that great day at the end of time recorded by John** saying, *I saw an angel come down from heaven, having the key of the bottomless pit and a great chain in his hand. And he laid hold on the dragon, that old serpent, which is the Devil, and Satan, and bound him a thousand years, And cast him into the bottomless pit, and shut him up, and* set a seal upon him, that he should deceive the nations no more.[514]

Sun Stands Still: Second Coming

As was the account of Sodom, so was the account of Israel in the days of Joshua. In the days leading up to the destruction of Sodom, two angels entered Sodom to measure the people. Likewise, two messengers were sent into Jericho to measure the sins of the people. Both cities were found worshipping other gods. In both cases, the Lord gave Israel victory over the kings of the land. Both were destroyed with great hail. While the great hail fell upon Israel's enemies, Joshua called upon the Lord and said *in the sight of Israel, Sun, stand thou still upon Gibeon.* 119 **And**

---

[510] Leviticus 16:8-10.
[511] Revelation 19:20; 20:10, 14, 15.
[512] Matthew 28:18.
[513] Joshua 10:16-18.
[514] Revelation 20:1-3.

<u>**the sun stood still**</u>**...** *until the people had avenged themselves upon their enemies... So* <u>*the sun stood still*</u> *in the midst of heaven, and hasted not to go down about a whole day.*[515] 120 Likewise, when **the sun was risen upon the earth** *...Then the LORD rained upon Sodom and upon Gomorrah brimstone and fire from the LORD out of heaven; And he overthrew those cities, and all the plain, and all the inhabitants of the cities, and that which grew upon the ground.*[516] 121 And both accounts point to the **outpouring of the great hail of the last plague at the end of time** as recorded by John where it says, *there fell upon men a great hail out of heaven, [every stone] about the weight of a talent: and men blasphemed God because of the plague of the hail; for the plague thereof was exceeding great.*[517]

These are yet other important symbolic transforms of events! And these events, like so many others are connected by the helical wave form of time. But the sands of time are fast running out.

And of the very last days John said, *And I saw an angel* <u>*standing in the sun*</u>*; and he cried with a loud voice, saying to all the fowls that fly in the midst of heaven, Come and gather yourselves together unto the supper of the great God; That ye may eat the flesh of kings, and the flesh of captains, and the flesh of mighty men, and the flesh of horses, and of them that sit on them, and the flesh of all [men, both] free and bond, both small and great.*[518] These accounts all faithfully record the Second Coming of the Sun of Righteousness when the last plague is poured out of the seventh vial. It is then that the final victory will be accomplished over Satan, death, and the grave.

---

[515] Joshua 10:12, 13.
[516] Genesis 19:23-25.
[517] Revelation 16:21.
[518] Revelation 19:17, 18.

Joshua Takes Over for Moses

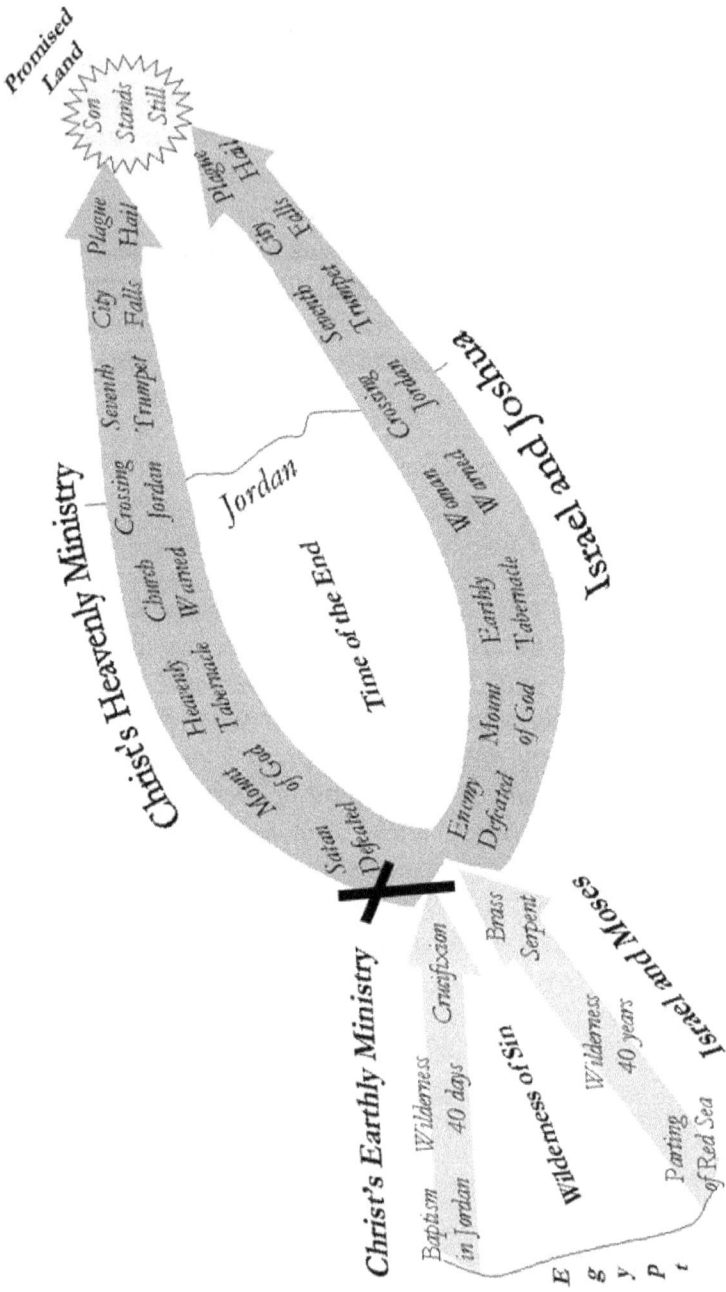

Promised Land

Son Stands Still

Plague Hail

City Falls

Seventh Trumpet

Crossing Jordan

Woman Warned

Earthly Tabernacle

Mount of God

Enemy Defeated

Israel and Joshua

Plague Hail

City Falls

Seventh Trumpet

Crossing Jordan

Church Warned

Heavenly Tabernacle

Mount of God

Satan Defeated

Christ's Heavenly Ministry

Jordan

Time of the End

Christ's Earthly Ministry

Baptism in Jordan

Wilderness 40 days

Crucifixion

Brass Serpent

Wilderness of Sin

Wilderness 40 years

Israel and Moses

Parting of Red Sea

Egypt

Sanctuary Steps of Jesus

1   **SACRIFICE FOR SINS:** Jesus Sacrificed in the **Court**

2   **RESURRECTION DAY:** Jesus (High Priest) takes the blood of His Sacrifice into the Holiest Place for acceptance by God (Revelation 5); Jesus Returns to the Court (Road to Emmaus; Luke 24)

3   **DAILY SACRIFICES: Jesus Ascends and Crosses the Veil into Holy Place (Mark 16:19)**

4   Jesus Puts Oil in the Golden Candlesticks (Pentecost)

5   Bread of the Presence Is renewed every Sabbath

6   Altar of Incense: incense is mingled with the Blood of Jesus to make prayers acceptable (Revelation 8:4)

7   **DAY OF ATONEMENT: Jesus crosses the Veil into the Holiest Place Once (Revelation 11:19)**

8   Messenger (angel) warnings (Revelation 14:7-9, 18)

9   Jesus sits with the Father as Judge (Daniel 7:13)

10   All the People from Adam to the Present Come before the Throne for Consideration

11   Jesus intercedes for Each Person with His Blood and blots sins out of the Book of Life

12   **PROBATION IS CLOSED: (Revelation 15:5, 8) all are Judged, Jesus our High Priest leaves the Holiest Place:** Jesus our High Priest cleanses the sanctuary

13   **LEAVES SANCTUARY: Jesus changes clothes now Captain of the Lord's Host as King of Kings and Lord of Lords and Leaves the Holy Place**

14   The sins placed on the Scapegoat fall on the wicked as the Plagues (Revelation 15:6-8; 16)

15   **SECOND COMING OF JESUS (Revelation 19:11-16)**

16   Sin destroyed and burned in Fire (Revelation 20)

17   **GOD TABERNACLES WITH MAN**

Promised Land: Heaven

In the days that followed the last plague, the inheritance that was promised to Abraham was fulfilled. All the tribes of 122 **Israel received their inheritance**. So shall it be in the time of the end. And Joshua *took a great stone, and set it up there under an oak, that [was] by the sanctuary of the LORD.*[519] And that great stone points to Jesus, our Rock. And the Oak stands for His Cross where He sacrificed all for the remission of our sins. And Jesus stands before the sanctuary made without hands in the heavens forever. AMEN.

Sanctuary Stage: Reverse Helix

The travels of Israel follow the Sanctuary Stage as if it were a template. In each key event, Israel is tied to an object on the Stage. The Court represents the world including Sodom and Egypt, where also our Lord was crucified.[520] We see the opening of the Red Sea represented by the veil to the Holy Place and the laver which symbolizes baptism. We see the three objects of the Holy Place (Golden Candlesticks, Table of Shewbread, and the Altar of Incense) as symbols of burning bush, the manna, and Mount Horeb. We also see the opening of the Jordan represented by the opening of the veil to the Holiest Place[521] where the people must pass before the Ark of the Covenant, just as the people of Israel passed before the Ark in the Jordan. Importantly, we see the cycle that we are in today. And that cycle is represented by the steps of Jesus in the Heavenly Sanctuary. Those that accept Jesus (2) are baptized (3) and begin a cycle of studying the Word (5, Shewbread), sharing the new Light (4, Candlesticks), and praying to God (6, Altar of Incense). Jesus is now sealing His people in front of the Ark of the Covenant (7) before Judgment closes. The fate of all will be final when the Door to the Ark is closed.

---

[519] Joshua 24:26.
[520] Revelation 11:8.
[521] Revelation 11:19.

Sanctuary Stage: Key to Israel's Travel

Promised Land
Holiest Place

Jericho

Mount Zion

Veil to Holiest Place

Jordan Opens

Dead Sea

7b Ark in Jordan

Travel of Israel

Sanctuary Key

Deliberately Reversed

1		Court
2	Brazen Altar	
3a	Brazen Laver	
3b		Holy Place
5	Table of Shewbread	
	7 Golden Candlesticks	
4	Altar of Incense	
6		Holiest Place
7a 7b	Ark of the Covenant	

Manna

Mount Sinai 6 (Horeb)

Burning Bush

Holy Place

Veil to Holy Place Red Sea Opens

Red Sea

Baptism

Passover Sacrifice

Court

E G Y P T

Israel Guided by the Sanctuary Pattern

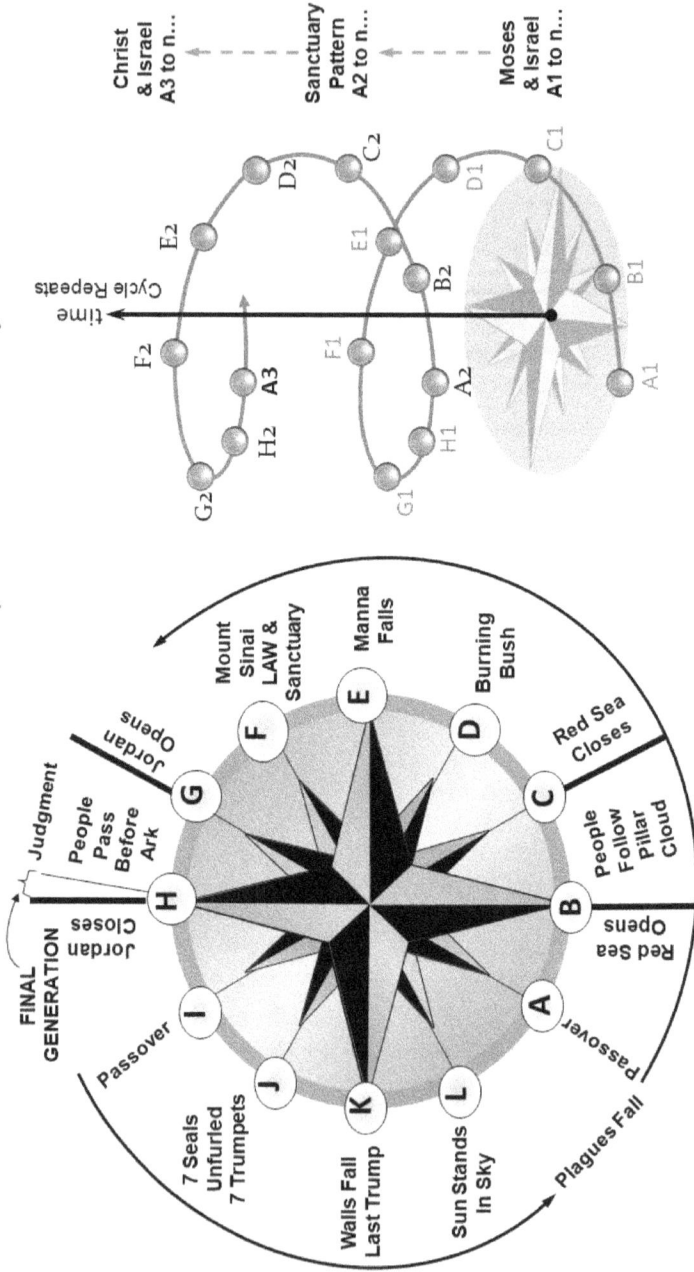

Christ & Israel A3 to n…

Sanctuary Pattern A2 to n…

Moses & Israel A1 to n…

time

Cycle Repeats

A1, B1, C1, D1, E1, F1, G1, H1, A2, B2, C2, D2, E2, F2, G2, H2, A3

Mount Sinai LAW & Sanctuary

Manna Falls

Burning Bush

Red Sea Closes

People Follow Pillar Cloud

Red Sea Opens

Passover

Plagues Fall

Sun Stands In Sky

Walls Fall Last Trump

7 Seals Unfurled 7 Trumpets

Passover

Jordan Closes

FINAL GENERATION

Jordan Opens

Judgment

People Pass Before Ark

A, B, C, D, E, F, G, H, I, J, K, L

CLOSING ARGUMENTS

Wherefore seeing we also are compassed about with so great a cloud of witnesses, let us lay aside every weight, and the sin which doth so easily beset [us], and let us run with patience the race that is set before us, Looking unto Jesus the author and finisher of [our] faith; who for the joy that was set before him endured the cross, despising the shame, and is set down at the right hand of the throne of God.[522]

How could events in the lives of so many people of the Old Testament parallel the events in the life of Christ, hundreds to more than a thousand years before His birth? How is it that even the path that Israel took from Egypt to the Promised Land parallels the events of the Revelation of John? From a scientific point of view these events were not by coincidence. They were determined in advance to provide us with shadows, types, and patterns (ensamples) of the future! But no man can write the future in advance. All things work together for good to them that love God, to ***them who are the called*** *according to [his] purpose. For whom he did foreknow, he also did predestinate [to be] conformed to the image of his Son.[523]*

---

[522] Hebrews 12:1, 2.
[523] Romans 8:28, 29.

11   *Closing Arguments: Summing up the Testimony*

We shall all stand before the judgment seat of Christ. For it is written [as] I live, saith the Lord, every knee shall bow to me, and every tongue shall confess to God. So then every one of us shall give account of himself to God. [524] Watch ye therefore, and pray always, that ye may be accounted worthy to escape all these things that shall come to pass, and to stand before the Son of man.[525]

Unimaginable forces are engaged in an invisible intergalactic war that has raged since the foundation of the world. And these formidable forces of darkness[526] and light[527] dwarf anything mankind can fathom or invent. In the deepest recesses of time, legions of evil demons were cast out of Heaven[528] to planet Earth, the prized possession of Jesus, the Prince of Light.[529] It is right here on Earth, that Jesus created mankind, His crowning Creation, in His own likeness.[530] But once expelled from heaven, Abaddon,[531] the prince of darkness, set forth a new plan to steal the prized creation of Earth by taking mankind captive as a stepping stone to retake the Heavenly Throne of God. And from the very first skirmish on Earth, the prince of darkness toppled the innocence of mankind through treachery, lies, and deception, and claimed Earth as his captive Kingdom. But a secret plan to take back the kingdom, had been set in motion by the

---

[524] Romans 14:10-12.
[525] Luke 21:36.
[526] Ephesians 6:12.
[527] 2 Kings 6:17.
[528] Revelation 12:9.
[529] John 8:12.
[530] Genesis 1:26.
[531] Revelation 9:11.

Prince of Light and His Father, before the foundation of the world.[532]   And the Plan was hidden in plain sight, that all that placed their allegiance to the Prince of Light would find it. But the same plan has long been hidden and kept secure, from those that would harm the Kingdom, by the **Guardians, Keepers of God's Secret Code.** Imagine a supernatural code that can differentiate the nature of a person's mind and heart!

The Judge that sitteth upon the throne is innocent of all charges brought before the heavenly Court by the fallen Lucifer, the covering cherub, that we now know as Satan. Long ago, Satan stood with Christ before the throne but he became the *accuser of the brethren.*[533] I can hear Jesus saying, *How art thou fallen from heaven, O Lucifer, son of the morning?...For thou hast said in thine heart, I will ascend into heaven, I will exalt my throne above the stars of God: I will sit also upon the mount of the congregation... I will ascend above the heights of the clouds; I will be like the most High.*[534]

Satan's pride grew to immeasurable proportions as he watched Christ create the Earth and mankind. Satan knew from the beginning that God entrusted the Government into Christ's hands.[535] Because of his pride and lust for the power of the throne, Satan intended to take the control of the government from Christ. Hoping to raise himself above Christ, he falsely accused the Father of instituting a LAW of government that cannot be kept.   Through false reports and deceit Satan convinced the heavenly hosts that he should replace God as the head of the government[536] of Creation. Satan is so corrupted by his jealousy and lust for power, that he brought forth *evil thoughts, murders, adulteries, fornications, thefts, false witness, [and] blasphemies[537]* to the kingdom. Satan falsely persuaded a third of the angels[538] that God's LAW limits

---

[532] Matthew 13:35; Hebrews 9:26.
[533] Revelation 12:10.
[534] Isaiah 14:12-14.
[535] Isaiah 22:21.
[536] Isaiah 9:6, 7.
[537] Matthew 15:19.
[538] Revelation 12:4, 9.

the freedoms of the heavenly hosts. He promised a better form of government.

Based on the testimony of the Two Witnesses,[539] Jesus demonstrates to the Highest Court, that Satan's ways lead to misery, death, and the grave. Satan's initial accusations turned many from God by dissuading them that God is a God of Love. But Christ's death on the Cross proves that God is Love[540] and that God's LAW does not limit freedom; it is the *perfect LAW of liberty*.[541] *For this is the love of God, that we keep his commandments: and his commandments are not grievous.*[542] And Satan and the fallen angels *shall be judged by the law of liberty. For he shall have judgment without mercy, that hath showed no mercy; and mercy rejoiceth against judgment.*[543]

The very accusations that have been brought against the Throne, are false. The testimonies of the Guardians prove that Satan is the origin of all of the misery that has been brought about in Heaven and on Earth. *Oh let the wickedness of the wicked come to an end; but establish the just: for the righteous God trieth the hearts and reins.*[544] In *the defense of God,* the revealed code demonstrates that Satan works *with iniquity, and hath conceived mischief, and brought forth falsehood. He made a pit, and digged it, and is fallen into the ditch [which] he made.* The very accusations that he has brought into the Highest Court belong upon his own head. *His mischief shall return upon his own head, and his violent dealing shall come down upon his own pate.* [545]

---

[539] Two Witnesses: the Old and New Testaments. Testimonies of God's Love.
[540] 1 John:5:3; 4:16.
[541] James 1:25.
[542] 1 John 5:3.
[543] James 2:12, 13.
[544] Psalms 7:9.
[545] Psalm 7:10, 14, 15.

12 *War in Heaven*

And there was war in heaven: Michael and his angels fought against the dragon; and the dragon fought and his angels, And prevailed not; neither was their place found any more in heaven. And the great dragon was cast out, that old serpent, called the Devil, and Satan, which deceiveth the whole world: he was cast out into the earth, and his angels were cast out with him.[546]

Our God is a God of Love, *merciful and gracious, longsuffering, and abundant in goodness and truth, keeping mercy for thousands, forgiving iniquity and transgression and sin...and that will by no means clear [the guilty].*[547] Satan saw himself as more than Christ's equal, even more deserving of the throne than Jesus or even God the Father. And when Satan learned that the Father and the Son planned to create man in their own image, his jealousy was inflamed. His pride had grown so great that he became jealous and angered because the Father had not consulted him in their plan of Creation. Satan could not accept that Jesus had alone been given the authority to command the government of the Universe, arguing that he was more deserving than the I AM. Satan's pride drove him to rebel against the government of God. He purposed to overthrow the government of God and take the throne because he was unwilling to submit to the authority that God had bestowed upon the Son. God determined that the case made by Satan was dangerously unwarranted and ordered that Satan and his followers be quarantined. Satan's pride led to conflict, and a War in Heaven broke out and in the end *that old serpent, called the Devil, and Satan, which deceiveth the whole world: he was cast out into the earth, and his angels were cast out with him.*[548] As the account of Joseph attests, Jesus brought the evil report to Israel, the Ancient

---

[546] Revelation 12:7-9.
[547] Exodus 34:6, 7.
[548] Revelation 12:9.

of Days; the very God of Israel that sits upon the throne. Jesus sits at the right hand of God the Father, garbed in the rainbow of light as a coat of many colors.

The Garden: Picture of Heaven

The Godhead had to win by Love and Satan took advantage of their character. But little did Satan know that the Garden of Eden is a living stage that foreshadows the Plan of Salvation. It was born of *things which have been kept secret from the foundation of the world*.[549] Most importantly, the Garden was designed as a test stage upon which the real character of Satan would be revealed. Symbolic imagery abounds in the illustration of the Garden. It provides a stage which reflects the beauty of heaven itself. The Godhead placed the first man, made in their Image, in the Garden. They also confined Satan and his fallen angels to the same planet. And it was there that the Universe watched as Satan plotted the downfall of Adam. And Satan sought to kill anyone that might be the Redeemer, the Seed, the Savior down through the ages from Adam and Eve to Jesus. Satan was allowed to carry out his evil plan so that the entire Universe could see to what lengths he would go if he and his angels had been allowed to displace the Government of God or even remain in Heaven. The Godhead also allowed the contagion of sin, brought by Satan to run its course, that all would not be misled by his lies and deceptions, and witness Satan's true intentions. The actions of Satan leave no doubt of his character and the wickedness that would have befallen Heaven if he had not been cast to Earth. For it is written, *Woe to the inhabiters of the earth and of the sea! for the devil is come down unto you, having great wrath, because he knoweth that he hath but a short time*.[550] The entirety of the Universe would have been in jeopardy. Likewise, it is in the Garden, that the righteousness and Love of God is revealed through the Plan to save humanity by love. How do you win a war of violence with LOVE?

---

[549] Matthew 13:35.
[550] Revelation 12:12.

Prophetic Turning-point

Satan brought about death through sin, as it is recorded, **the wages of sin [is] death; but the gift of God [is] eternal life through Jesus Christ our Lord.**[551] After Satan caused the downfall of mankind, the outcome of the War was revealed to the Universe. God spelled out the consequences of Satan's actions saying, **I will put enmity between thee and the woman, and between thy seed and her seed; it shall bruise thy head, and thou shalt bruise his heel. Unto the woman he said, I will greatly multiply thy sorrow and thy conception; in sorrow thou shalt bring forth children; and thy desire [shall be] to thy husband, and he shall rule over thee. And unto Adam he said, Because thou hast hearkened unto the voice of thy wife, and hast eaten of the tree, of which I commanded thee, saying, Thou shalt not eat of it: cursed [is] the ground for thy sake; in sorrow shalt thou eat [of] it all the days of thy life; Thorns also and thistles shall it bring forth to thee; and thou shalt eat the herb of the field; In the sweat of thy face shalt thou eat bread, till thou return unto the ground; for out of it wast thou taken: for dust thou [art], and unto dust shalt thou return.**[552]

Satan's tactics became clear for, **he was a murderer from the beginning, and abode not in the truth, because there is no truth in him. When he speaketh a lie, he speaketh of his own: for he is a liar, and the father of it**.[553] Satan caused the first couple to fall because he told them the lie of lies: **Ye shall not surely die: For God doth know that in the day ye eat thereof, then your eyes shall be opened, and ye shall be as gods, knowing good and evil.**[554] It was this same character, born of envy and jealousy that caused the War in Heaven and death to the inhabitants of Earth. None of his accusations are true. In the end, God will be exonerated and the Universe will once again be freed forever of sin.

---

[551] Romans 6:23.
[552] Genesis 3:15-19.
[553] John 8:44.
[554] Genesis 3:4, 5.

Rivers Cross at the Tree of Life

The Godhead intentionally planted two trees at the center of the garden, *the tree of life also in the midst of the garden, and the tree of knowledge of good and evil.*[555] These two trees are planted at the Crossing of four rivers that take the water of life to the far reaches of the Garden. The Crossing rivers represent the Cross where Jesus was crucified. The four rivers come from the fountain that flows from Jesus. The two trees symbolize Satan and Christ. These are the two opponents that bring the War to a decisive moment at the Cross. Satan, represented by the tree of knowledge of good and evil, will be removed forever as seen in the vision of John who says, *And he showed me a pure river of water of life, clear as crystal, proceeding out of the throne of God and of the Lamb. In the midst of the street of it, and on either side of the river, [was there] the tree of life.*[556] In the end, Satan, represented by **the tree of knowledge of good and evil will be uprooted forever**. Only the Tree of Life, a symbol of Jesus, will remain in the New Jerusalem. Satan, the covering cherub that once stood beside the throne in heaven, will be no more. The fountain of waters that flow in all directions symbolize the living waters, the very waters that flowed from the Rock in the wilderness, the same cleansing waters of the Jordan, the same healing waters that flowed from Christ's side when He was pierced upon the Cross.

Bridegroom and the Church

Adam was the first symbolic Bridegroom. Eve was the first symbol of his bride, the church. Because Adam was not strong enough to withstand the wiles of Satan, Jesus was sent to rescue mankind as the Scriptures say, *for as in Adam all die, even so in Christ shall all be made alive.*[557] And so it is written, *the first man Adam was made a living soul; the last Adam [was made] a*

---

[555] Genesis 2:9.
[556] Revelation 22:1, 2.
[557] 1 Corinthians 15:22.

quickening spirit. Howbeit that [was] not first which is spiritual, but that which is natural; and afterward that which is spiritual. The first man [is] of the earth, earthy: the second man [is] the Lord from heaven.[558] For Jesus is the spiritual Bridegroom who is come to rescue the Bride.

Lamb Slain from the Foundation

Adam and Eve realized that sin brought about their nakedness. The robes of light that once graced them while they walked the garden in innocence were gone. Their fate of death was sealed. But through Christ's death they would be given the opportunity to be restored to eternal life. This was established by giving them skins for coverings, symbols of the robes of the ***Lamb slain from the Foundation of the World***[559] that their birthright might be restored. Likewise, Jacob went before his father Isaac wearing the skin of a goat upon his arm.[560] Jacob was given the birthright because he wore the skin as his substitute. In the same manner, you and I can wear the covering of Jesus, the Lamb slain from the foundation of the world, and be restored to our eternal home.

Leaves for Healing or Death

The leaves on the two trees are symbolic of the character and love of Jesus in contrast to the pride of Satan. The Tree of Life is the WORD. ***The leaves of the tree [are] for the healing of the nations.*** In other words, every page of the WORD that we refer to as the Bible, emanates the love of God for the healing of the people. On the other hand, the leaves on the Tree of Knowledge of Good and Evil bring about death. Satan's character is reflected in that tree. Just as its fruit brought about the death of mankind, so will it's leaves. Its leaves are words that twist the thoughts of men to evil. The knowledge, encouraged by Satan, takes men

---

[558] 1 Corinthians 15:45-47.
[559] Revelation 13:8.
[560] Genesis 27:21-23.

unwittingly away from a sense of need for God. They are led to believe that they surely will not die with the knowledge of Satan's tree. Science and medicine cannot give us eternal life.

The Ark Preserves the Way

The Garden of God foreshadows the heavenly Sanctuary. The two trees at the cross of the four great rivers symbolize the Altar in the Sanctuary. And the fountain represents the cleansing water of the laver, like the cleansing waters of the Jordan. And as in the Sanctuary, there are two covering cherubim on either side of the Shekinah Glory like *a flaming sword which turned every way, to keep the way of the tree of life*.[561] Jesus, the Light of the World is like a flaming sword turning in all directions, like a lighthouse that guides those in darkness home. For as Joshua testified, all must pass before the Ark of the Covenant to make their Way back home. And the flaming sword is the WORD of God which shines for everyone that seeks. The Sanctuary of forgiveness of sins is open today. And to those that seek Jesus, it is written, *Ask, and it shall be given you; seek, and ye shall find; knock, and it shall be opened unto you*.[562] The flaming sword preserves the way home.

The Justice of God

It is also written, *He that rejecteth me, and receiveth not my words, hath one that judgeth him: the word that I have spoken, the same shall judge him in the last day.*[563]

---

[561] Genesis 3:24.
[562] Luke 11:9, 10.
[563] John 12:48.

13 *Miracle Birth*

In the beginning was the Word, and the Word was with God, and the Word was God. The same was in the beginning with God. And the Word was made flesh, and dwelt among us...[564]

Many miracle babies point forward to the birth of Christ including Isaac, Jacob, Joseph, Samson, Samuel, Moses, Solomon, and John the Baptist. Each miracle account is used in harmony with the others by the Divine Author to weave a more complete foreshadowing of the birth of Jesus. Several are used here to show that each of these work together, to collectively point to the miracle birth of Jesus. Evidence of the circumstances surrounding Christ's birth were made abundantly clear in the writings of *the law of Moses, and the Prophets and the Psalms concerning [Jesus].*[565]

The Divine Stage was set in the Garden by God's prophetic decree.[566] Satan would be destroyed by the Seed of the woman. *Now the parable is this: The Seed is the Word of God.*[567] And *in the beginning was the Word, and the Word was with God, and the Word was God. The same was in the beginning with God. And the Word was made flesh, and dwelt among us...*[568] And so it was that the Seed, known as the WORD, would condemn and destroy Satan. The Divine Seed was passed down from the woman in the Garden and sprouted and yielded the Christ Child at the appointed time.[569] It was the Godhead's Plan from the very beginning, that Jesus would be made *a little lower than the*

---

[564] John 1:1, 2, 14.

[565] Luke 24:44.

[566] Genesis 3:15.

[567] Luke 8:11.

[568] John 1:1, 2, 14.

[569] Daniel 9:24-27. The prophecy states that the Messiah will appear before the Jerusalem and its sanctuary are destroyed (in 70AD).

angels[570] and *that through death He might destroy him that had the power of death, that is, the devil; For verily He took not on Him the nature of angels; but He took on Him the seed of Abraham.*[571] The WORD hid the Seed that was passed from Adam[572] through Abraham[573] and David[574] in plain sight to protect the Plan. From the very beginning, Jesus was destined to save the world and defeat Satan through love. And *greater love hath no man than this, that a man lay down his life for his friends.*[575]

Satan, fearful of the prophecy given in the Garden, attacked, and even murdered those that might bear the Seed. Satan would kill the unrighteous and righteous man alike. None, no not one, would be safe if Satan were to continue to reign on Earth. *He was a murderer from the beginning, and abode not in the truth, because there is no truth in him.*[576] And so it was that Satan worked through Cain to murder Abel. And *death reigned from Adam to Moses, even over them that had not sinned after the similitude of Adam's transgression, who is the figure of him that was to come.*[577] Christ's offering was the only hope for mankind; no other offering would suffice. So it is said, *Lo, I come (in the volume of the book it is written of me,) to do thy will, O God. He taketh away the first* [sacrifices and burnt offerings], *that he may establish the second. By the which will we are sanctified through the offering of the body of Jesus Christ once [for all].*[578]

The visit of Gabriel to Mary and Joseph was foreshadowed by the appearance of the Angel of the Lord first to Samson's mother, and then to his father. The angels directed that both Samson and Jesus were to be holy and set apart. Samson would be a Nazarite which pointed to Christ's birth in Nazareth. But also in the Hebrew,

---

[570] Psalm 8:5.
[571] Hebrews 2:14-16.
[572] Luke 3:38.
[573] Luke 3:34.
[574] Matthew 1:1.
[575] John 15:13.
[576] John 8:44.
[577] Romans 5:14.
[578] Hebrews 10:5-10; Psalms 40:6-8.

Nazareth[579] points to the Branch. And Jesus the Messiah is the Branch spoken of by the prophets.[580] Gabriel, was sent to Mary, saying *Hail, [thou that art] highly favoured, the Lord [is] with thee: blessed [art] thou among women. Fear not, Mary: for thou hast found favour with God. And, behold, thou shalt conceive in thy womb, and bring forth a son, and shalt call his name JESUS. He shall be great, and shall be called the Son of the Highest: and the Lord God shall give unto him the throne of his father David...*[581] Later, Gabriel would announce Christ's birth to Mary's husband, Joseph.[582] So the birth announcements would be made first to the mother, then to the father.

Christ's birth was also foreshadowed by the announcement of the birth of Isaac by the Angel of the Lord. And Jesus is that Angel of the Lord, that is accompanied by His two angels.[583]

Before Christ's birth, his parents left Nazareth and travelled to Bethlehem to pay taxes. Bethlehem was the birth place of King David who pointed also to Christ's birthplace.[584] And by going there, the prophecy spoken of by the prophet Micah was fulfilled. *But thou, Bethlehem Ephratah, [though] thou be little among the thousands of Judah, [yet] out of thee shall he come forth unto me [that is] to be ruler in Israel; whose goings forth [have been] from of old, from everlasting.*[585] At Christ's birth, wise men had travelled from the orient where the writings of Moses, Daniel, and others had long been studied. When they saw Christ's sign in the sky,[586] they joyfully followed the star to Jerusalem, expecting a huge celebration. But there was none. So they inquired of the people and of Herod, seeking the place of Christ's birth. In a rage Herod, feeling mocked of the wise men when they asked to be directed to the place where Christ was born, charged his own chief

---

[579] *Netzer*, root of the word Nazareth means Branch.
[580] Isaiah 11:1; Jeremiah 23:5; 33:15; Zechariah 3:8; 6:12.
[581] Luke 1:28-35.
[582] Matthew 1:20.
[583] Genesis 19:1; John 20:12.
[584] 1 Samuel 16:4.
[585] Micah 5:2.
[586] Numbers 24:17. Star out of Jacob.

priests and scribes to give him the name of the place. *And they said unto him, In Bethlehem of Judaea: for thus it is written by the prophet...*[587] Satan had worked through Pharaoh who *charged all his people, saying, Every son that is born ye shall cast into the river...*[588] This event pointed to circumstances surrounding the death decree at Christ's birth that was foreshadowed by the birth of Moses. As it is written, *then Herod, when he saw that he was mocked of the wise men, was exceeding wroth, and sent forth, and slew all the children that were in Bethlehem, and in all the coasts thereof, from two years old and under, according to the time which he had diligently inquired of the wise men.*[589]

Christ was wrapped in grave cloths at His birth[590] and the Magi presented Him with gold, frankincense, and myrrh. Christ's ultimate mission was to free mankind from sin and death, and so the swaddling clothes and myrrh[591] pointed to His death, burial, and resurrection. The gold pointed to His kingship as King of Kings and the frankincense pointed to His Divinity.[592] Like Moses, His parents sent Him to Egypt, for refuge to escape the murderous king. This was so *that it might be fulfilled which was spoken of the Lord by the prophet, saying, Out of Egypt have I called my son.*[593] Now all these things fulfilled the words of the prophet saying, *For unto us a child is born, unto us a son is given: and the government shall be upon his shoulder: and his name shall be called Wonderful, Counsellor, The mighty God, The everlasting Father, The Prince of Peace. The Lord sent a Word into Jacob, and it hath lighted upon Israel.*[594]

All the miracle births work together to pinpoint the birth of Jesus.

---

[587] Matthew 2:5.
[588] Exodus 1:22.
[589] Matthew 2:16.
[590] Luke 2:7, 12.
[591] Genesis 37:25; Matthew 2:11.
[592] Exodus 30:34-38.
[593] Hosea 11:1; Matthew 2:15."
[594] Isaiah 9:6-8.

Creation

War in heaven

From Heaven to Incarnation

He Sees — Advance
Future in — Coat
Rainbow Controversy, — Envy
Mission to go to Sheep of Israel
Crosses Vale

Joseph, Savior of the World

Angel Announces — Mother — Father — Birth
Miracle Birth
Holy Child — Nazarite

Samson, All Powerful, Omnipotent Deliverer

Born in Bethlehem Descends from Abraham
Son of Jesse
Shepherd

David, King of Kings

Children Murdered at His birth — Adopted Son — Hidden In Egypt

Moses, the Law Giver

The Lord and Angels Announce Birth Descends from Abraham

Isaac, the Sacrifice
Immanuel **God with Us** — Miracle Virgin Birth — Birth **Bethlehem** — Born in from David — Descends **Tribe of Judah** — Root of Jesse

70 week prophecy

Children Murdered Rachel Crying — **Called out of Egypt**

Son of Adam
SEED of the Woman — War, Enmity with Satan — **Scepter shall not depart from Judah**

The Prophets
God within the womb

Will be King of the Jews — **Line of David**

The Psalms

Second Adam — Messiah Cut-off Midst of Week
3.5 years

14 *The Temptation*

Watch and pray, that ye enter not into temptation: the spirit indeed [is] willing, but the flesh [is] weak.[595] *For this purpose the Son of God was manifested, that he might destroy the works of the devil.*[596] *...And when the devil had ended all the temptation, he departed from him for a season.*[597]

Temptation has fallen upon all of mankind. The Divine Author weaves a more complete foreshadowing of the temptation of Jesus through several Old Testament accounts, just as he wove together the miracle births. Satan deceitfully misquotes God's Word as his means of ensnaring men. *He was a murderer from the beginning, and abode not in the truth, because there is no truth in him. When he speaketh a lie, he speaketh of his own: for he is a liar, and the father of it.*[598] The verses of the WORD of God are to be used by us, as a sword to counter Satan and drive him away, at least for a season. *For we wrestle not against flesh and blood, but against principalities, against powers, against the rulers of the darkness of this world, against spiritual wickedness in high [places]... Above all, taking the shield of faith, wherewith ye shall be able to quench all the* <u>*fiery darts of the wicked.*</u> *And take the helmet of salvation, and* <u>*the sword of the Spirit, which is the word of God..*</u>[599]

---

[595] Matthew 26:41; Mark 14:38; Luke 4:13.
[596] 1 John 3:8.
[597] Luke 4:13.
[598] John 8:44.
[599] Ephesians 6:12-17.

Pride and Power

For Adam and Eve, the temptation came down to three points as it did for Jesus. *When the woman saw that the tree [was] good for food, and that it [was] pleasant to the eyes, and a tree to be desired to make [one] wise, she took of the fruit thereof, and did eat, and gave also unto her husband with her; and he did eat.*[600] After 40 days, Christ's human body was in an emaciated state. He craved for food and Satan could see that He was weakened and hungered for food. As he had tempted Adam and Eve, Satan also tempted Jesus by offering His desperately starved body with food saying, *If thou be the Son of God, command that these stones be made bread.*[601] But Jesus knew that Satan was mocking Him by saying *IF thou be the Son of God*. Satan insinuated that Jesus might not be the Son of God. Satan put Jesus on trial but Jesus *answered and said, It is written, Man shall not live by bread alone, but by every word that proceedeth out of the mouth of God.*[602] On the second point, Satan showed Jesus a vista that was exceedingly beautiful to behold. He took Jesus to the top of the temple and again said, *IF thou be the Son of God, cast thyself down: for it is written, He shall give his angels charge concerning thee: and in [their] hands they shall bear thee up, lest at any time thou dash thy foot against a stone.* To which Jesus responded, *It is written again, Thou shalt not tempt the Lord thy God.*[603] And for the final test, Satan took Jesus on a high mountain and brought before Christ's view, the kingdoms of the world and said, *All these things will I give thee, IF thou wilt fall down and worship me.*[604] When Jesus heard that Satan would have Him bow down to him, Jesus replied in disgust saying, *Get thee hence, Satan: for it is written, Thou shalt worship the Lord thy God, and him only shalt thou serve.*[605]

---

[600] Genesis 3:6.
[601] Matthew 4:3.
[602] Matthew 4:4.
[603] Matthew 4:5-7.
[604] Matthew 4:8-9.
[605] Matthew 4:10.

The Spirit moved upon Samson to point to Christ's encounter with Satan in the wilderness. Of Samson, it is said, *the spirit of the LORD began to move him...*[606] These words point to the Words found in the account of Jesus, *Then was Jesus led up of the Spirit into the wilderness to be tempted of the devil.*[607] Samson was led into the wilderness to face the roaring lion because the Lord *sought an occasion against the Philistines: for at that time the Philistines had dominion over Israel.*[608] Likewise, Jesus was led by the Spirit to oppose Satan. Satan, was convinced that because of Christ's human frailty, He would fall prey to sin like all other men. But Christ overcame sin giving proof that He was the Worthy[609] Sacrifice. As it is written, *For verily he took not on [him the nature of] angels; but he took on [him] the seed of Abraham. Wherefore in all things it behoved him to be made like unto [his] brethren, that he might be a merciful and faithful high priest in things [pertaining] to God, to make reconciliation for the sins of the people. For in that he himself hath suffered being tempted, he is able to succour [aid] them that are tempted.*[610] Christ's human form suffered unimaginably and was in severe distress, and yet, if Jesus had failed upon a single point, Satan would wield his evil power over the Earth henceforth.

The account of David and Goliath is deliberately provided in the Scriptures to illuminate events surrounding Christ's temptation on the grand stage of the Universe. Both David and Jesus are Shepherds of the flock of Israel. Both David and Jesus are anointed as the *Beloved* of the Father. Both David and Jesus are chosen to be the worthy King of Israel; David of physical Israel, and Jesus the King of Kings of spiritual Israel. In the days of David, Israel had been occupied by the foreign invaders of Philistine. In Christ's days, spiritual Israel had been invaded with the supernatural forces of Satan. The army of David's Israel stood upon one mountain and the Philistines stood upon another with a

---

[606] Judges 13:25.
[607] Matthew 4:1.
[608] Judges 14:4.
[609] Revelation 5:2, 12.
[610] Hebrews 2:16-18.

valley between. In Christ's account, the angels watched the spectacle from heaven while the demonic forces of Satan watched from their position on Earth with an unseen veil between the two. It was the same veil that hid the forces of Israel from the eyes of Elisha's servant.[611] The forces of Light met the forces of darkness on that field of battle. Goliath had accused Israel day and night, just as Satan accuses the brethren. The **supernatural contest would be enacted** by a soldier of Israel and Goliath of the Philistines. And before the engagement, Goliath set forth the conditions. **The losers would become the slaves of the winner. David came to the battle front with bread for Israel just as Jesus came with the WORD, the bread of life**. David's brethren didn't want his help. **They felt he was unworthy. Likewise, the Scribes and Pharisees of Israel didn't find Jesus worthy**. Goliath challenged Israel for forty days before David vowed to meet him. Likewise, Satan taunted Jesus day and night for 40 days until he was weak. **It was on the 40th day that David would face Goliath and Jesus would face Satan**. The King of Israel offered his daughter in marriage to the one who would defeat Goliath. Likewise, **the King of the Universe offered Israel as the bride of Christ if He would defeat Satan**. Goliath was a giant of a man, but Satan is far more imposing as an angel of darkness. No man could long stand before the wicked angel Satan, without Divine protection which is freely given to those that ask. **Goliath stands for evil, and Satan the devil is the epitome of evil.**

Few men appreciate the risk that was taken on that 40th day. **Had Jesus lost the battle, humanity would forever be shackled in darkness.** All would be forced to bow to Satan. David would face Goliath without the armor of men and David, like Jesus, would face the enemy with *righteousness as a breastplate, and an helmet of salvation upon his head; and he put on the garments of vengeance [for] clothing, and was clad with zeal as a cloak.*[612] **The Spirit of the Lord went with David and Jesus** and strengthened them. By all appearances, through the view of earthly eyes, **David and Jesus appeared to be at a serious**

---

[611] 2 Kings 6:17.
[612] Isaiah 59:17; Ephesians 6:14-17.

disadvantage. But in the eyes of the Lord, both were pure of heart and soldiers of the Lord. Goliath threatened David by saying, *I will give thy flesh unto the fowls of the air, and to the beasts of the field.*[613] But David and Jesus would be the ones that would feed the enemy to the *fowls of the air and the beasts of the field.*[614] Goliath would draw his giant sword against David just as Satan would draw his sword of lies against Jesus. But David would take pebbles from the brook, just as Jesus would take pebbles from the Rock of the spiritual brook, pebbles that are verses from the WORD of God, to defeat the enemy. **The battle would be the Lord's**, for the Lord is mighty in battle. And **the pebble of David sank into the forehead of Goliath just as the verses of the WORD of God penetrated the mind of Satan.** *It is written, Man shall not live by bread alone, but by every word that proceedeth out of the mouth of God.*[615] *For the word of God [is] quick, and powerful, and sharper than any two-edged sword, piercing even to the dividing asunder of soul and spirit, and of the joints and marrow, and [is] a discerner of the thoughts and intents of the heart.*[616] On the 40th day the head of the Philistines was defeated just like the head of Satan's angelic forces was defeated. And **upon the 40th day** David and Jesus secured the freedom of Israel from the oppression of the wicked one. In the end, David was surrounded by the camp of Israel, just as Jesus was encircled by the angels of heaven.[617]

As the angelic armies watched Christ's encounter, His worthiness became apparent. Satan would use treachery, deception, and lies. Christ would defeat Satan and his demons with the WORD of God. Jesus proved to the heavenly Court, that God's Laws can be obeyed. To fend against Satan's army, Jesus gave us His *angels charge over [us], to keep [us] in all [our] ways. They shall bear thee up in [their] hands, lest thou dash thy foot against a stone.*[618] *And He gives us His Sword, the WORD of LIFE.*

---

[613] 1 Samuel 17:44.
[614] 1 Samuel 17:46; Revelation 19:17, 18.
[615] Matthew 4:4.
[616] Hebrews 4:12.
[617] Matthew 4:11.
[618] Psalm 91:11, 12.

15 *Ministry: World on Fire*

If our gospel be hid, it is hid to them that are lost: In whom the god of this world hath blinded the minds of them which believe not, lest the light of the glorious gospel of Christ, who is the image of God, should shine unto them. For we preach not ourselves, but Christ Jesus the Lord; and ourselves your servants for Jesus' sake. For God, who commanded the light to shine out of darkness, hath shined in our hearts, to [give] the light of the knowledge of the glory of God in the face of Jesus Christ.[619]

Satan's accusations that the governance of the Universe under God's LAW is unfair was never his real motive. It was just an excuse to rally angels to sympathize with him so that he could achieve his real objective. And that objective has always been to take the throne of the Universe from God.[620] *He was a murderer from the beginning, and abode not in the truth, because there is no truth in him. When he speaketh a lie, he speaketh of his own: for he is a liar, and the father of it.*[621] He is the *accuser of the brethren*,[622] shamelessly and falsely accusing the innocent, to bring them under his subjection. In his conspiracy to tempt Christ, he even went so far as to tempt Christ to bow to him,[623] just as he attempted to get Mordecai to bow to Haman. *And when Haman saw that Mordecai bowed not, nor did him reverence, then was Haman full of wrath.*[624] Haman's anger pointed forward in time to the 40 day temptation of Jesus by Satan. Like Haman before him, Satan was outraged when Jesus refused to bow down and worship him. If Jesus had accepted Satan's *tempting proposal*, He would have sinned and the *wages of sin are death*. Had Jesus fallen, Satan would have triumphed and the

---

[619] 2 Corinthians 4:3-6.
[620] Isaiah 14:13, 14.
[621] John 8:44.
[622] Revelation 12:10.
[623] Matthew 4:8, 9; Luke 4:7.
[624] Esther 3:5.

Universe would have been his alone. But in the end, the tables were turned on Haman as they will be turned on Satan and *his mischief shall return upon his own head, and his violent dealing shall come down upon his own pate.*[625]

After the temptation, **Satan retreated with his forces to implement an even more devious and deadly plan to maintain his reign over the kingdom of Earth and to secure the throne of God.** His plot was to corrupt those that were in Christ's inner circles and use Christ's own brethren to tempt Jesus and to kill Him just as Satan caused the brethren of Joseph to plot to kill him.[626] When Jesus told His disciples that *[He] must be killed, and after three days rise again,* Satan personally entered Peter. Satan thought he could play on Christ's emotions through Peter saying, *Be it far from thee, Lord: this shall not be unto thee.* It was then that Jesus looked at Peter, and saying to Satan that had entered into Peter, *Get thee behind me, Satan: for thou savourest not the things that be of God, but the things that be of men.*[627] Satan used the ancient lie from the Garden saying, *Ye shall not surely die,*[628] to tempt Jesus. And Satan was the one that later gave the order to execute Jesus, for it is written, *then entered Satan into Judas surnamed Iscariot, being of the number of the twelve.*[629] Satan and his forces were body snatchers, entering the bodies and minds of men, twisting their thoughts and deeds for Satan's evil purposes.

Likewise, Satan worked to cloud and darken the understanding of the Scriptures so that even the very elect should not understand the light that had been given to the priests, scribes, and Pharisees of Israel. These were the very ones that had been entrusted with the hidden meanings of the writings that *must be fulfilled, which were written in the law of Moses, and [in] the prophets, and [in] the psalms, concerning [Jesus].*[630] In their darkness, the house of

---

[625] Psalm 7:16.
[626] Genesis 37:20.
[627] Matthew 16:22, 23; Mark 8:31-34.
[628] Genesis 3:4.
[629] Luke 22:3.
[630] Luke 24:44.

Israel rejected Jesus, though the evidence was clear, because the veil of Satan covered their hearts and minds.[631]

Christ's objective is to save.[632] Satan's objective is to destroy.[633] After the 40 day period of temptation, *Jesus returned in the power of the Spirit into Galilee.*[634] And when Jesus arrived at Nazareth, *He went into the synagogue on the sabbath day and stood up to read.* Jesus picked up a scroll and read, *The spirit of the Lord GOD [is] upon me; because the LORD hath anointed me to preach good tidings unto the meek; he hath sent me to bind up the brokenhearted, to proclaim liberty to the captives, and the opening of the prison to [them that are] bound; To proclaim the acceptable year of the LORD, and the day of vengeance of our God; to comfort all that mourn; To appoint unto them that mourn in Zion, to give unto them beauty for ashes, the oil of joy for mourning, the garment of praise for the spirit of heaviness; that they might be called trees of righteousness, the planting of the LORD, that he might be glorified.*[635] After Jesus read that passage in the synagogue, Satan's angels enraged the scribes and Pharisees and they took Jesus to a cliff to cast Him down[636] but it was not yet His time. The very ones of Christ's own house, were overcome by the darkness of Satan and they didn't even know that the long awaited Redeemer stood before them!

From the onset of His ministry, Jesus knew that forces of innumerable demonic angels had taken over the minds and bodies of the human race, just as they had before the Flood. Their numbers are more than ten thousand times ten thousand and thousands of thousands. Mankind cannot withstand the fallen angels without the aid of the Spirit.[637] Satan's intent is to imprison the people of Earth and hold them hostage in darkness to his wicked ways of sin and death. He was the one that tempted them

---

[631] 2 Corinthians 3:15.
[632] John 3:17.
[633] Jeremiah 4:7; 1 Corinthians 10:10.
[634] Luke 4:14.
[635] Isaiah 61:1-3; Luke 4:18, 19.
[636] Luke 4:29.
[637] Ephesians 6:13.

to bow down to false idols like the golden calf in the wilderness, the great statue in Babylon, and Dagon of Nineveh and Ashdod.[638] When the people bowed, they unwittingly bowed to Satan, and Satan mocked them and sneered at them. Satan's abuse of the people is but a glimpse of a Universe that he would govern. It was well within Christ's power to take the Kingdom of Earth back by force but that would have undermined the case for God. It was Christ's mission to restore the kingdom through LOVE alone.[639]

Set the World on Fire

Satan's forces had taken innumerable prisoners by inflicting illness and holding them hostage. Those that held God's precious scrolls, had been blinded and knew not that the battle raged about them. One woman had been crippled and bent for eighteen years and Jesus went to heal her on the Sabbath day. The head of the synagogue spoke against Him with indignation whence Jesus replied, ***ought not this woman, being a daughter of Abraham, whom Satan hath bound, lo, these eighteen years, be loosed from this bond on the sabbath day?***[640] What better day is there for a miracle to drive Satan away from a victim than on the Lord's Day?

Jesus selected 12 apostles and 70 disciples just as Moses had selected 12 and 70 before Him. Jesus would build His army around them. They would be Christ's warriors that would fight without hands, but rather would defeat the enemy with the WORD that He would give them. ***For the word of God [is] quick, and powerful, and sharper than any two-edged sword, piercing even to the dividing asunder of soul and spirit, and of the joints and marrow, and [is] a discerner of the thoughts and intents of the heart.***[641] Jesus sent them into the fields to confront the enemy.

---

[638] 1 Samuel 5:1-12.
[639] 1 John 4:16.
[640] Luke 13:10-16.
[641] Hebrews 4:12.

For the field is the world[642] and the fire within the twelve was the indwelling of the Holy Spirit.[643]

Likewise, Samson sent them into the fields two by two[644] just as Jesus did and they set the field on fire. Likewise, Jesus sent the Twelve *saying, Go not into the way of the Gentiles, and into [any] city of the Samaritans enter ye not: But go rather to the lost sheep of the house of Israel. And as ye go, preach, saying, The kingdom of heaven is at hand. Heal the sick, cleanse the lepers, raise the dead, cast out devils: freely ye have received, freely give.*[645] It was an all out confrontation between the forces of good and evil. *And they went out, and preached that men should repent. And they cast out many devils, and anointed with oil many that were sick, and healed [them].*[646] It is the Spirit of Christ working through His WORD, that gives us power over **Legions**[647] **of fallen**

---

[642] Matthew 13:38.
[643] Judges 15:14; Acts 2:3, 4.
[644] Mark 6:7; Judges
[645] Matthew 10:5-8.
[646] Mark 6:12, 13.
[647] Mark 5:9.

angels. The Spirit that led Christ's apostles and disciples is the same Spirit that led Jesus into the wilderness to confront Satan.[648] It is the same Spirit that protects us!

Conquerors of Untold Thousands

The warfare throughout the Holy City had risen to a violent pitch when Jesus went to the hillsides and fed and ministered to the 5000 and the 4000. The multiplying of the loaves and fishes was to soothe the hunger pains of their bodies; the preaching was to free them from the bondage of Satan. Jesus and His followers had been in deadly warfare with Satan's forces from the time war broke out in heaven. But the warfare is not of flesh and blood. *For though we walk in the flesh, we do not war after the flesh: (For the weapons of our warfare [are] not carnal, but mighty through God to the pulling down of strong holds;) Casting down imaginations, and every high thing that exalteth itself against the knowledge of God, and bringing into captivity every thought to the obedience*[649] *of Christ*. Demons had entered into the people like a contagion.[650] Yet Christ's WORD set the captives free and they were reborn to newness of life.[651] Thousands were *being born again, not of corruptible seed, but of incorruptible, by the word of God, which liveth and abideth for ever.*[652]

The warfare that took place in the days of Samson and David was earthly[653] yet the sacred text pointed to the spiritual warfare that Christ's forces waged. Had the learned ones of the Scribes and Pharisees rightly discerned the meaning of the accounts of Samson[654] and David,[655] they would have learned of this great Spirit warfare. Yes, Samson slayed thousands with the jawbone of

---

[648] Matthew 4:1.
[649] 2 Corinthians 10:3-5.
[650] Luke 8:30.
[651] Romans 6:4, 5.
[652] 1 Peter 1:23.
[653] John 3:31.
[654] Judges 13 – 16.
[655] 1 Samuel 18:27.

an ass. But *jawboning* points to the spiritual death wrought by speaking or preaching. The sacred text says that Samson killed them with the jawbone and then ended speaking![656]

The manner by which Samson killed his thousands points to the way that Jesus converted thousands. As the text says, *knowing this, that our old man is crucified with [him], that the body of sin might be destroyed, that henceforth we should not serve sin. For he that is dead is freed from sin.* Jesus slayed thousands with His WORD that they died of the old man and were reborn.[657] The sacred text testifies of this, for it says he killed them *hip and thigh*. Could anyone kill thousands physically by hitting them upon their hip and thigh alone? This was the clue, for had they known the Scriptures, they would have known that this was explained in the writings of Moses where it says, The Angel of the Lord changed Jacob by touching him on the hip and thigh and he was changed from Jacob, which means thief, to Israel which means overcomer. Everyone that hears Christ's WORD has

[656] Judges 15:17.
[657] Ephesians 4:21-24; 2 Corinthians 5:17; Romans 6:6, 7.

the choice to be born again, just as Jacob, and be an overcomer of sin and death. Likewise, the text says that Saul killed his thousands and David his ten thousands. And again the text unveils the deeper meaning because it says David brought back their foreskins.[658] And foreskins are a symbol of circumcision. For it is written, *circumcise therefore the foreskin of your heart, and be no more stiffnecked.*[659] *And the LORD thy God will circumcise thine heart, and the heart of thy seed, to love the LORD thy God with all thine heart, and with all thy soul, that thou mayest live.*[660] All that follow Jesus must have a circumcision of the heart.[661]

The accounts of Samson and David symbolize the supernatural warfare between Christ and Satan. For more than three years Christ's forces drove out thousands upon thousands of evil angels from the bodies and minds of men. Victory upon victory was won even though Christ was hounded by Satan's forces, just as David was hunted and forced into hiding. In victory, Jesus sent disciples to John saying, *Go your way, and tell John what things ye have seen and heard; how that the blind see, the lame walk, the lepers are cleansed, the deaf hear, the dead are raised, to the poor the gospel is preached.*[662] Miracles were wrought, even greater than in the days of Moses and Elisha. In the end, Satan retreated into the city as if it were his last stronghold and he plotted to kill Jesus there. Satan corrupted the holy people that Jesus had entrusted with the sacred writings *and the chief priests and scribes sought how they might kill Him.*[663]

Again the Divine Author weaves a more complete foreshadowing of the ministry of Jesus through several Old Testament accounts, just as he wove together the miracle births and the Temptation. It was deliberately done to provide PROOF of the existence of GOD.

---

[658] 1 Samuel 18:27; Jeremiah 4:4; Deuteronomy 30:6; Romans 2:29.
[659] Deuteronomy 10:16.
[660] Deuteronomy 30:6.
[661] Jeremiah 4:4; Romans 2:29.
[662] Luke 7:22.
[663] Luke 22:2.

16 *Triumphal Entry*

O clap your hands, all ye people; shout unto God with the voice of triumph. For the LORD most high [is] terrible; [he is] a great King over all the earth. He shall subdue the people under us, and the nations under our feet.[664] [And] having spoiled principalities and powers, ... triumphing over them ...[665]

T he war with Satan had finally come to a tumultuous turning point. The people saw the earthly manifestations of these supernatural battles. They saw as Christ and His followers freed those possessed from their demons; they saw the blind and the deaf healed; and they saw the lame walk and the sick healed. And several days prior to Christ's Triumphal entry into Jerusalem, many witnessed the raising of Lazarus from the dead. The people could sense the culmination of a momentous event. Rumors spread that He was the long expected Messiah[666] and that He was about to set up His throne in Jerusalem. Jesus did come as the Messiah and He would take the throne in accordance with the Scriptures. He would not establish His throne in physical Jerusalem until the end of time. He would suffer, be crucified, be buried, and ascend as the King of Kings to His heavenly throne.

After Jesus raised Lazarus from the dead, He set out with His disciples for Jerusalem because the time appointed was fast approaching. As they approached Bethphage and Bethany, Jesus sent two of His disciples out to retrieve a colt[667] that He should ride into the City as the long awaited King. As Jesus looked down over the beautiful City from Olivet, He realized that in the days

---

[664] Psalm 47:1-3.
[665] Colossians 2:15.
[666] Daniel 9:24-27.
[667] Luke 19:29-31.

and hours that followed He would fulfill hundreds of prophecies written of old. He could hear Zechariah's words saying, *Rejoice greatly, O daughter of Zion; shout, O daughter of Jerusalem: behold, thy King cometh unto thee: he [is] just, and having salvation; lowly, and riding upon an ass, and upon a colt the foal of an ass.*[668] The Plan to rescue mankind had been choreographed many times in advance in Old Testament accounts. The fulfillment of events would document and vindicate God the Father. As Jesus looked over the City, He could see the place where Abraham and Isaac arrived at the foot of the Hill with their colt and two servants; pointing to the two that rolled back the Gate of the Tomb. Father and the Son would climb to the summit alone where the sacrifice would take place. Isaac would carry the wood on his back just as Jesus would later carry the wood on His.[669] A ram with thorns on its head would be provided as the substitute for Isaac just as Jesus would be the sacrificial substitute with a crown of thorns on His head, for the redemption of mankind. John had aptly called Jesus *the Lamb of God which taketh away the sins of the world.*[670]

Jesus turned and looked at the Sheep Gate where the sacrificial lamb for the nation of Israel would be selected on that very day; the tenth day of Nisan. Jesus would be that Passover Lamb.[671] Jesus would be without a blemish of sin[672] just as the Passover lamb was to be without blemish. His bones would not be broken[673] just as the bones of the Passover lamb were not to be broken. The blood of Jesus was shed though He was innocent,[674] just as the Passover lamb's was innocent blood. And just as the blood of the Passover Lamb would cover the door posts in Egypt, Christ's blood would stain the Cross and would be freely offered to protect the people of Israel by covering their hearts and minds.[675]

---

[668] Zechariah 9:9.
[669] Genesis 22:5, 6.
[670] John 1:29.
[671] 1 Corinthians 5:7.
[672] 2 Corinthians 5:21.
[673] John 19:36.
[674] Matthew 27:4, 24; Jonah 1:14; Jeremiah 26:15; 1 Samuel 19:5.
[675] Hebrews 13:12.

Jesus rode the colt into Jerusalem to signify His Kingship and to fulfill the account of the transfer of the Kingdom from David to Solomon. Just as Moses and Joshua represent a divine pairing of Christ's earthly and heavenly presence, David represents Christ's earthly presence and Solomon represents Christ's heavenly presence. Just as Joshua takes Israel to the Promised Land and Solomon becomes their Judge, so does Jesus lead Spiritual Israel into the Promised Land across Jordan where Jesus resides today as the Judge of Israel. In order to fulfill the succession, Jesus overcame Satan just as Solomon overcame his rivals for the throne.[676] Both were anointed and both won the victory without the shedding of the blood of others. Their thrones would be greater than the throne of their Father, King David.[677] Solomon rode upon King David's mule and Jesus rode upon the young colt. Both were destined to be Kings of Israel. As they rode, their processions were accompanied by great rejoicing. *And the multitudes that went before, and that followed, cried, saying, Hosanna to the son of David: Blessed [is] he that cometh in the name of the Lord; Hosanna in the highest.*[678] And the noise was so great, that the whole City of Jerusalem heard their processions and it is written, *the people piped with pipes, and rejoiced with great joy, so that the earth rent with the sound of them.*[679] And in both cases the opposition leaders wanted to know who they were, saying, *wherefore [is this] noise of the city being in an uproar?*[680] Both were sons of David.[681] Both would ascend to the throne. With the passing of David, Solomon ascended to his throne in Zion. After Christ's resurrection, He ascended to His throne in the heavenly Zion. Solomon would judge the people of Israel from his throne[682] just as Jesus judges the world from His heavenly throne.

As Jesus came near the City, He wept over it because His beloved people were blind to the grave danger they would soon face. Their

---

[676] 1 Kings 1:37-46.
[677] 1 Kings 1:37.
[678] Matthew 21:9.
[679] 1 Kings 1:40.
[680] 1 Kings 1:41.
[681] Matthew 1:1, 20; 21:9.
[682] 1 Kings 1:46.

eyes were blinded by Satan and they knew not the hidden secrets of the Scriptures. The Scriptures recorded their fate saying, *thine enemies shall cast a trench about thee, and compass thee round, and keep thee in on every side, and shall lay thee even with the ground, and thy children within thee; and they shall not leave in thee one stone upon another; because thou knewest not the time of thy visitation.*[683] And it is written, *the people of the prince that shall come shall destroy the city and the sanctuary.*[684] And all this came to pass just as it is written. As the procession proceeded on its *descent of the mount of Olives, the whole multitude of the disciples began to rejoice and praise God with a loud voice for all the mighty works that they had seen; Saying, Blessed [be] the King that cometh in the name of the Lord: peace in heaven, and glory in the highest. And some of the Pharisees from among the multitude said unto him, Master, rebuke thy disciples. And He answered and said unto them, I tell you that, if these should hold their peace, the stones would immediately cry out.*[685]

And when the procession entered into Jerusalem, all the city was moved, saying, Who is this? And the multitude said, This is Jesus the prophet of Nazareth of Galilee.[686] He came as *the Lamb of God that taketh away the sins of the world*; He was the *last Adam*, the One that would *bruise the head of the serpent*; and He would be the One proclaimed by Isaiah saying the *government shall be upon his shoulder: and his name shall be called Wonderful, Counsellor, The mighty God, The everlasting Father, The Prince of Peace.* And Satan's angels say, *Let [us] alone; what have we to do with thee, thou Jesus of Nazareth? art thou come to destroy us? I know thee who thou art, the Holy One of God.*[687] It was then that Jesus said, *Now is the judgment of this world: now shall the prince of this world be cast out.*[688]

---

[683] Luke 19:42-44. Also see Matthew 24:2.
[684] Daniel 9:26.
[685] Luke 19:37-40.
[686] Matthew 21:10, 11.
[687] John 1:29; 1 Corinthians 15:45; Genesis 3:15; Isaiah 9:6; Mark 1:24.
[688] John 12:31.

17 *Tempest: World on Trial*

He will laugh at the trial of the innocent. The earth is given into the hand of the wicked: he covereth the faces of the judges thereof; if not, where, [and] who [is] he?[689] Beloved, think it not strange concerning the fiery trial which is to try you, as though some strange thing happened unto you: But rejoice, inasmuch as ye are partakers of Christ's sufferings; that, when his glory shall be revealed, ye may be glad also with exceeding joy.[690]

S ince the day that Jesus gave the evil report to His Father in heaven, Satan has been working relentlessly to undermine the LAW and government of the Universe through false witness, slander, deceit, treachery, ruthlessness, deception, blasphemy, malice, cruel deeds, and even murder. From the days of Adam, he purposed to destroy the Promised Seed. He so corrupted the generations from Adam

---

[689] Job 9:23, 24.
[690] 1 Peter 4:12, 13.

to Noah that *the wickedness of man [was] great in the earth, and [that] every imagination of the thoughts of his heart [was] only evil continually.*[691] After the Flood, it was Satan that polluted Israel with idol worship. And over the centuries it was Satan that murdered the prophets and burned the martyrs. *And others had trial[s] of [cruel] mockings and scourgings, yea, moreover of bonds and imprisonment: They were stoned, they were sawn asunder, were tempted, were slain with the sword: they wandered about in sheepskins and goatskins; being destitute, afflicted, tormented; (Of whom the world was not worthy): they wandered in deserts, and [in] mountains, and [in] dens and caves of the earth.*[692] Even at Christ's birth *the dragon stood before the woman which was ready to be delivered, for to devour her child as soon as it was born.* And at Christ's Triumphal Entry into Jerusalem, Satan purposed to stop His sinless walk. In his rage, Satan decided to accomplish this by putting Jesus through such cruel agony that Satan believed that Jesus, Himself, would end the crucifixion and lose the Kingdom.

Soon after the Triumphal Entry, Satan turned Christ's trusted apostle against Him. *And the chief priests and scribes sought how they might kill Him; for they feared the people. Then entered Satan into Judas surnamed Iscariot, being of the number of the twelve. And he went his way, and communed with the chief priests and captains, how he might betray Him unto them.*[693] Jesus foresaw that Satan would use His advisor because, Ahithophel, David's trusted advisor had betrayed him. **Both of their advisors hung themselves.** Christ's soul fainted because of Satan's relentless attacks. It is written, *Now is my soul troubled; and what shall I say? Father, save me from this hour: but for this cause came I unto this hour. Father, glorify thy name. Then came there a voice from heaven, [saying], I have both glorified [it], and will glorify [it] again. The people therefore, that stood by, and heard [it], said that it thundered: others said, An angel spake to him. Jesus answered and said, This voice*

---

[691] Genesis 6:5.
[692] Hebrews 11:36-38.
[693] Luke 22:2-4.

came not because of me, but for your sakes. Now is the judgment of this world: now shall the prince of this world be cast out.[694]

Satan caused Jerusalem to be in an uproar like a tempest upon the sea. He stirred the hearts of the Pharisees and Sadducees to jealousy. And with Christ's entry into Jerusalem, Satan continuously agitated the leaders to kill Him. The tempest that afflicted Jonah pointed to this very time in history. Jonah paid the price and entered upon his journey. Similarly, Jesus entered upon His journey to pay the price and redeem His people. Unseen enemy angels stirred up the crowds that had travelled to Jerusalem. These demons were as *raging waves of the sea, foaming out their own shame; wandering stars, to whom is reserved the blackness of darkness forever.*[695] These evil angels were the ones that led *Judas, one of the twelve, and with him a great multitude with swords and staves, from the chief priests and the scribes and the elders.*[696] They took Jesus prisoner not knowing that it was through Jesus that *the scriptures must be fulfilled.*[697]

From the Garden of Gethsemane to Calvary, Jesus began to bear the Gate of the tomb just as Samson had carried the Gate to the top of the hill. This was done that the *Gates of Hell shall not prevail.*[698] For the Gates of Hell are the doors to the tomb. Jesus was on a mission to remove the doors to the grave.

Jesus was taken to the Roman authorities to be prosecuted. *Pilate entered into the judgment hall again, and called Jesus, and said unto Him, Art thou the King of the Jews? … Jesus answered, My kingdom is not of this world: if my kingdom were of this world, then would my servants fight, that I should not be delivered to the Jews: but now is my kingdom not from hence. Pilate therefore said unto Jesus, Art thou a king then? Jesus answered, Thou sayest that I am a king. To this end was I born, and for this cause came I into the world, that I should bear witness unto the truth.*

---

[694] John 12:27-31.
[695] Jude 1:13.
[696] Mark 14:43.
[697] Mark 14:49; Matthew 26:52-56.
[698] Matthew 16:18.

Pilate saith unto Jesus, What is truth? And when he had said this, he went out again unto the Jews, and saith unto them, I find in him no fault [at all].[699] Likewise, the account of Jonah pointed to Christ's Trial because the captain of the ship asked Jonah the same questions that Pilate asked Jesus. The Captain of the ship knew the seas well enough that he knew that the tempest was supernatural. Pilate knew from his wife's dream that the supernatural was involved. **Both asked, Why has this evil fallen upon us? What is your occupation? They are both prophets. Where do you come from? They are both Galileans. What is your country? They are both from Israel. What people are you from? They are both Hebrews. What shall we do to calm the sea? They both had to be sacrificed to calm the sea.**[700] The Captain of Jonah's ship and Pilate (like the pilot of a ship) both concluded that the blood of Jonah and Jesus was **innocent blood.**[701] And **neither "Captain" could find fault with them.**[702] And as the storm arose the mariners aboard Jonah's ship panicked and tried to row ashore.[703] Likewise, the mariners that travelled with Jesus were concerned for their lives and they were scattered like sheep.[704] This fulfilled the words of the prophet, saying,[705] *I saw all Israel scattered upon the hills, as sheep that have not a shepherd.*

Satan and his fallen demons enraged the crowd and preyed on the pride of the religious leaders. And it is written, *Pilate answered them, saying, Will ye that I release unto you the King of the Jews? For he knew that* <u>*the chief priests had delivered him for envy.*</u> *But the chief priests moved the people, that he should rather release Barabbas unto them. And Pilate answered and said again unto them, What will ye then that I shall do [unto him] whom ye call the King of the Jews? And they cried out again, Crucify him. Then Pilate said unto them,* <u>*Why, what evil*</u>

---

[699] John 18:33-38
[700] Jonah 1:8-12.
[701] Jonah 1:14; Matthew 27:24.
[702] Luke 23:22.
[703] Jonah 1:13.
[704] Mark 14:27.
[705] 1 Kings 22:17.

hath he done? And they cried out the more exceedingly, Crucify him.[706] *Pilate saith unto them, Take ye him, and crucify [him]: for I find no fault in him. The Jews answered him, We have a law, and by our law he ought to die, because he made himself the Son of God. When Pilate therefore heard that saying, he was the more afraid; And went again into the judgment hall, and saith unto Jesus, …knowest thou not that I have power to crucify thee, and have power to release thee? Jesus answered, Thou couldest have no power [at all] against me, except it were given thee from above: therefore he that delivered me unto thee hath the greater sin.*[707]

And [so] Pilate, willing to content the people, released Barabbas unto them, and delivered Jesus, when he had scourged [him], to be crucified.[708] It was the only way that Pilate could calm the sea of humanity. It was the only way that the Captain of Jonah's ship could calm the seas. Satan made a mockery of the trial…It is said, *He will laugh at the trial of the innocent. The earth is given into the hand of the wicked: he covereth the faces of the judges thereof; if not, where, [and] who [is] he?*[709]

---

[706] Mark 15:9-14.
[707] John 19:6-11.
[708] Mark 15:15.
[709] Job 9:23, 24.

18   *Three Days and Nights: Death, Burial, Resurrection*

Master, we would see a sign from thee. But he answered and said unto them, An evil and adulterous generation seeketh after a sign; and there shall no sign be given to it, but the sign of the prophet Jonas: For as Jonas was three days and three nights in the whale's belly; so shall the Son of man be three days and three nights in the heart of the earth.[710]

The Divine Author of the Scriptures provides an incredibly detailed chronicle of the events surrounding the death, burial, and resurrection of Jesus. A great cloud of witnesses testify of Jesus but the testimonies of the 7 Guardians and numerous other witnesses provide an overwhelming testament. The events in the lives of each of these 7 witnesses bear testimonies of Christ's life, death, burial, and resurrection. When assembled together as the pieces of a puzzle, their testimonies provide a detailed account of Christ's victory over death and sin. Yet their chronicles were recorded hundreds of years in advance. How can this be explained? There is only one explanation. They were deliberately and supernaturally documented in advance as evidence of Christ's sacrifice for those that can hear and see. Jesus said, *For I tell you, that many prophets and kings have desired to see those things which ye see, and have not seen [them]; and to hear those things which ye hear, and have not heard [them].* They reveal the account of the events of Christ's life in great detail and **they also reveal the evil actions taken by Satan** to undermine the Plan.

The weave is an exceptionally detailed PROOF of the existence of the supernatural, and the existence of GOD. WHY? Because the fate of all the worlds of the Universe were in jeopardy at the Cross. Satan tried to dissuade Christ from carrying out His mission by

---

[710] Matthew 12:38-40.

casting great delusions upon Him. Satan was using these vivid delusions to make the Cross unbearable for Jesus. In Christ's darkest moments, Satan tried to convince Jesus that He would be eternally separated from God[711] by the mountain of sin that engulfed Him. And Satan would again tempt Jesus at His weakest moments on the Cross saying, *Thou that destroyest the temple, and buildest [it] in three days, save thyself. If thou be the Son of God, come down from the cross. Likewise, also the chief priests mocking Jesus, with the scribes and elders, said, He saved others; himself he cannot save. If he be the King of Israel, let him now come down from the cross, and we will believe him.*[712] But through it all, Jesus knew that the almost unbearable pain inflicted upon His mind and body was coming from Satan himself. When Jesus heard them say **IF**, He knew that the voice He heard was that of Satan. It was the same voice Jesus had heard in the temptation. It was the same "IF" question that Satan asked Eve in the Garden. Despite Christ's pain there was no turning back. Too much was at stake.

During the days leading to the trial and His crucifixion, burial, and resurrection, Jesus made it abundantly clear to His apostles and disciples that He must be crucified *saying, The Son of man must suffer many things, and be rejected of the elders and chief priests and scribes, and be slain, and be raised the third day.*[713] The Old Testament Scriptures repeat the circumstances surrounding Christ's death, burial, and resurrection in clear manner, numerous times, yet Satan and his demons so darkened the eyes and dulled the minds of the religious leaders that they did not know Jesus, nor how and why He should die. The writings of Moses, and the psalms[714] and the prophets[715] all *testify of [Jesus].*[716] Yet the very ones Jesus entrusted to carry the holy messages to the world were

---

[711] Isaiah 59:2.
[712] Matthew 27:40-42.
[713] Luke 9:22.
[714] Psalm 22.
[715] Isaiah 53.
[716] John 5:39; Luke 24:44.

ignorant and understood not what they read as *the blind gropeth in darkness.*[717]

When Jesus was approached by *certain of the scribes and of the Pharisees... saying, Master, we would see a sign from thee. But Jesus answered and said unto them, An evil and adulterous generation seeketh after a sign; and there shall no sign be given to it, but the sign of the prophet Jonas: For as Jonas was three days and three nights in the whale's belly; so shall the Son of man be three days and three nights in the heart of the earth.*[718] But they knew not the Scriptures because of Satan, *having [their] understanding darkened, being alienated from the life of God through the ignorance that is in them, because of the blindness of their heart...*[719]

Summation of the Evidence

Events of the circumstances surrounding Christ's death, burial, and resurrection are foreshadowed, step by step, through the accounts of the 7 witnesses. When studied carefully, with the help of the Spirit, they bear witness of these events written hundreds of years in advance. There is an overwhelming abundance of evidence but The following is a short summary of the testimony.

1. Before Christ's death, He entered Jerusalem as a King upon a colt. *All this was done, that it might be fulfilled which was spoken by the prophet, saying, Tell ye the daughter of Sion, Behold, thy King cometh unto thee, meek, and sitting upon an ass, and a colt the foal of an ass.*[720] *Rejoice greatly, O daughter of Zion; shout, O daughter of Jerusalem: behold, thy King cometh unto thee: he [is] just, and having salvation; lowly, and riding upon an ass, and upon a colt the foal of an ass.*[721]

---

[717] Deuteronomy 28:29.
[718] Matthew 12:38-40.
[719] Ephesians 4:18.
[720] Matthew 21:1-11
[721] Zechariah 9:9.

2. All this was foreshadowed by Solomon's triumphal entry into Jerusalem as he rode upon King David's mule.[722]

3. Jesus was presented to Israel as the sacrificial Passover lamb on the 10th day of Nisan, fulfilling the saying, *In the tenth [day] of this month they shall take to them every man a lamb, according to the house of [their] fathers, a lamb for an house.*[723] *the Lamb of God, which taketh away the sin of the world.*[724]

4. Upon Christ's entrance, the people said, *Blessed be he that cometh in the name of the Lord: We have blessed you out of the house of the Lord.*[725]

5. And the noise was so great that the whole City of Jerusalem heard the procession. It is written, *the people piped with pipes, and rejoiced with great joy, so that the earth rent with the sound of them.*[726]

6. Jesus would become the head of the heavenly temple thus fulfilling the saying, *The stone [which] the builders refused is become the head [stone] of the corner.*[727]

7. Jesus entered the temple and the little children came to Him, which fulfilled the saying, *Out of the mouth of babes and sucklings hast thou ordained strength because of thine enemies, that thou mightest still the enemy and the avenger.*[728]

8. Of the days before and after Christ's death it is said, *And in the days of these kings shall the God of heaven set up a kingdom, which shall never be destroyed: and the kingdom shall not be left to other people, [but] it shall break in pieces and consume all these kingdoms, and it shall stand for ever.*[729]

---

[722] 1 King 1:38.
[723] Exodus 12:3.
[724] John 1:29.
[725] Psalm 118:26.
[726] 1 Kings 1:40.
[727] Psalm 118:22.
[728] Psalm 8:2. Matthew 21:16.
[729] Daniel 2:44. Matthew 21:44.

9. Satan stirred the conflict between Christ and the Jewish leadership like a storm upon the seas of men.[730]

10. From the beginning of Christ's ministry, there were numerous plots and attempts by His brethren to kill Him.[731] These attempts were foreshadowed by plots to kill Joseph and David by their brethren, and Samson by those that opposed him.

11. The brethren of Moses plotted to stone him to death *saying, What shall I do unto this people? they be almost ready to stone me*[732]as a foreshadow of the plot to stone Jesus to death. These murderous plots were all directed by Satan as he influenced the minds of the religious leaders to kill Jesus.

12. The Pharisees, following the whispers of Satan, took counsel on how they might entangle Christ's talk[733] to fulfill the saying, *They also that seek after my life lay snares [for me]: and they that seek my hurt speak mischievous things, and imagine deceits all the day long.*[734]

13. But it was Jesus that entangled them by asking them, *What think ye of Christ? Whose son is he?*[735] When they said, *the Son of David*, Jesus confused them by asking them why David would call Him his Lord? How could Christ be both the Son of David[736] and the Father of David? He was both!

14. In those days the Pharisees and Sadducees were unfit to lead Christ's flock fulfilling the saying, *Whose possessors slay them, and hold themselves not guilty: and they that sell them say, Blessed [be] the LORD; for I am rich: and their own shepherds pity them not.*[737]

15. Jesus was a Refuge for the weary saying, *how often would I have gathered thy children together, even as a hen gathereth her chickens under [her] wings, and ye would not*! This fulfilled the saying of the prophet for Jesus is *a

---

[730] Jonah 1:4.
[731] Matthew 21:38.
[732] Exodus 17:4.
[733] Matthew 22:15.
[734] Psalm 38:12.
[735] Matthew 22:42, 43.
[736] Psalm 110:1.
[737] Zechariah 11:4-7.

hiding place from the wind, and a covert from the tempest, rivers of water in a dry place, as the shadow of a great rock in a weary land.[738]

16. Jesus would be sold for 30 pieces of silver fulfilling the words of the prophet saying, *So they weighed for my price thirty [pieces] of silver.*[739] Even His own brethren would betray Him for silver, as was the case in the accounts of Joseph, Samson, and Elisha.

17. Samson was betrayed by the woman which is a symbol of the church leadership that betrayed Jesus.

18. David was betrayed by Ahithophel, a trusted advisor just as Jesus was betrayed by Judas. This fulfilled the words of the prophet saying, *Yea, mine own familiar friend, in whom I trusted, which did eat of my bread, hath lifted up [his] heel against me.*[740] This was confirmed of Peter saying, *Men [and] brethren, this scripture must needs have been fulfilled, which the Holy Ghost by the mouth of David spake before concerning Judas, which was guide to them that took Jesus.*[741]

19. At the Passover meal, Jesus ushered in His new covenant which fulfilled the saying, *For the life of the flesh [is] in the blood: and I have given it to you upon the altar to make an atonement for your souls: for it [is] the blood [that] maketh an atonement for the soul.*[742]

20. Christ's new covenant was of the order of Melchizedek as it is written, *And Melchizedek king of Salem brought forth bread and wine: and he [was] the priest of the most high God.*[743]

21. Before they came for Jesus, He anguished in the Garden as it is written, *Draw nigh unto my soul, [and] redeem it: deliver me because of mine enemies. Thou hast known my reproach, and my shame, and my dishonour: mine*

---

[738] Isaiah 32:2.
[739] Zechariah 11:12.
[740] Psalm 41:9.
[741] Acts 1:16.
[742] Leviticus 17:11. Matthew 26:26-29.
[743] Genesis 14:18; Psalm 110:4; Hebrews 5:6, 10; 6:20; 7:1, 10-21.

adversaries [are] all before thee. Reproach hath broken my heart; and I am full of heaviness...[744]

22. Jesus began to carry the Gates of Hell to Calvary as foreshadowed by Samson who carried the Gate to the top of the Hill. This fulfilled the saying, the **Gates of Hell shall not prevail.** Men are captive to Satan and the grave. Jesus sets the captives free from sin and the grave.

23. Jesus was captured and taken from the Garden without a struggle so that it might be said, *He was oppressed, and he was afflicted, yet he opened not his mouth: he is brought as a lamb to the slaughter, and as a sheep before her shearers is dumb, so he openeth not his mouth.*[745]

24. Jonah was questioned by the Captain of the sea, and Jesus was questioned and tried by Pontius Pilate the Roman Governor with authority over the sea of people in Judea.

25. Jesus was falsely accused[746] as was Joseph. This fulfilled the words of the psalmist: *False witnesses did rise up; they laid to my charge [things] that I knew not.*[747]

26. Jesus was abused by His captors, fulfilling the words of the prophet, *I gave my back to the smiters, and my cheeks to them that plucked off the hair: I hid not my face from shame and spitting.*[748]

27. They took counsel against Jesus to kill Him as it is written, *while they took counsel together against me, they devised to take away my life.*[749]

28. As it is written, *the men that held Jesus mocked him, and smote [him]. And when they had blindfolded him, they struck him on the face...*[750] which was foreshadowed by the account of Samson who was blinded[751] and beaten.

29. Subsequently, Jesus was whipped, paraded before the people, and mocked. This was foreshadowed by the account

---

[744] Psalm 69:18-20.
[745] Isaiah 53:7.
[746] Matthew 26:59.
[747] Psalm 35:11.
[748] Isaiah 50:6.
[749] Psalm 31:13.
[750] Luke 22:63, 64.
[751] Judges 16:21.

of Samson where it says, *they called for Samson out of the prison house; and he made them sport...*[752]

30. Christ's betrayer, *cast down the pieces of silver in the temple, and departed, and went and hanged himself.*[753] This was foreshadowed in the account of David where it says, *when Ahithophel saw that his counsel was not followed, he saddled [his] ass, and arose, and gat him home to his house, to his city, and put his household in order, and hanged himself, and died, and was buried in the sepulchre of his father.*[754]

31. The religious leaders threw away the filthy lucre that was paid to sell Him out, fulfilling the words of the prophets saying, *Cast it unto the potter: a goodly price that I was prised at of them. And I took the thirty [pieces] of silver, and cast them to the potter in the house of the LORD.*[755]

32. Jesus was silent before His accusers, that the words of the prophet would be fulfilled saying, *But I, as a deaf [man], heard not; and [I was] as a dumb man [that] openeth not his mouth.*[756]

33. Jesus was despised and rejected which fulfilled the words of the prophets, saying, *my soul loathed them, and their soul also abhorred me.*[757] *He is despised and rejected of men; a man of sorrows, and acquainted with grief: and we hid as it were [our] faces from him; he was despised, and we esteemed him not.*[758]

34. Jesus was scourged with Roman whips that the words of the prophet would be fulfilled, *the plowers plowed upon my back: they made long their furrows.*[759]

35. Like Joseph, Jesus was stripped of His robe. *And they stripped him, and put on him a scarlet robe.*[760]

---

[752] Judges 16:25.

[753] Matthew 27:5.

[754] 2 Samuel 17:23.

[755] Zechariah 11:13; Jeremiah 32:7-9.

[756] Psalm 38:12.

[757] Zechariah 11:8;

[758] Isaiah 53:3.

[759] Psalm 129:3.

[760] Matthew 27:28.

36. Jesus was given a wooden cross to carry up to the mount. Likewise, Isaac carried the wood for the sacrifice on his back up to the top of **the same mount called Moriah**.

37. The Ancient of Days grieved for the Son when He looked upon the blood stained robe.[761] *Likewise, Christ's Father wept for Him.*

38. Christ's soul grieved as the time for the grave swiftly approached. His grief fulfilled the words of the psalmist saying, *For my soul is full of troubles: and my life draweth nigh unto the grave. I am counted with them that go down into the pit: I am as a man [that hath] no strength...*[762]

39. Jesus was sacrificed on the 14th of Nisan so that the foreshadowing of the Passover lamb in Egypt would be fulfilled. *And ye shall keep it up until the fourteenth day of the same month: and the whole assembly of the congregation of Israel shall kill it in the evening.*[763]

40. The blood on the beams of the Cross fulfilled the command of the Lord for the Passover Lamb. *They shall take of the blood, and strike [it] on the two side posts and on the upper door post of the houses.*[764]

41. The blood on the doorposts protected Israel in Egypt causing the Angel of Death to pass them by. Christ's blood, when it covers the heart, protects from eternal death. As it is written, *And to you who are troubled rest with us, when the Lord Jesus shall be revealed from heaven with his mighty angels, In flaming fire taking vengeance on them that know not God, and that obey not the gospel of our Lord Jesus Christ: Who shall be punished with everlasting destruction from the presence of the Lord, and from the glory of his power...*[765]

42. Jesus was nailed to the Cross so the words of the prophet would be fulfilled saying, *they pierced my hands and my*

---

[761] Genesis 37:31-35.
[762] Psalm 88:3, 4.
[763] Exodus 12:6.
[764] Exodus 12:7, 22.
[765] 2 Thessalonians 1:7-9.

feet.[766] And My heel was bruised as the prophecy foretold, saying, *thou [Satan] shalt bruise [Christ's] heel.*[767]

43. Like Absalom, Jesus was pinned by three darts; two in His hands and one in His feet.

44. *As Moses lifted up the serpent in the wilderness, even so must the Son of man be lifted up: that whosoever believeth in him should not perish, but have eternal life.*[768]

45. The serpent raised by Moses saved the people that had been bitten by the serpents in the wilderness if they would just look upon it. Likewise, the Cross was the antidote for the sins caused by the deadly bite of Satan and his serpents.

46. When Jonah was raised up, it calmed the tempest upon the sea. Likewise, when Jesus was raised up the sea of humanity was calmed.

47. When Absalom was caught up in the tree he was suspended between heaven and earth just as Satan was unwittingly suspended.

48. Jesus was thirsty and the words of the psalmist were fulfilled saying, *They gave me also gall for my meat; and in my thirst they gave me vinegar to drink.*[769]

49. They cast lots in the accounts of Jonah and Christ. Also, the words of the prophet were fulfilled saying, *They part my garments among them, and cast lots upon my vesture.*[770]

50. Jesus would be the great sacrificial substitute for many, just as the ram caught in the thicket was the substitute for Isaac.

51. They placed a crown of thorns on Christ's head just as Isaac's lamb was caught in a thicket of thorns that foreshadowed Christ's sacrifice as it is written, *and behold behind [him] a ram caught in a thicket by his horns: and Abraham went and took the ram, and offered him up for a burnt offering in the stead of his son.*[771]

52. Samson's arms were outstretched, pointing to Christ's stretched out arms.

---

[766] Psalm 22:16.
[767] Genesis 3:15.
[768] John 3:14, 15.
[769] Psalm 69:21.
[770] Psalm 22:18.
[771] Psalm 22:13.

53. The arms of Moses were outstretched, pointing to Christ's outstretched arms.

54. A fierce battle led by Joshua below the one with his hands outstretched[772] foreshadowed the battle between Christ's Spirit and the forces of darkness at the foot of the Cross.

55. Samson's hands were placed upon the two main pillars that held up the House of Dagon. The hands of Jesus would remove the two main pillars of Satan's synagogue: sin and death.

56. They placed a sign over Christ's head that read, *This is Jesus the King of the Jews*. This fulfilled the words of the prophet saying, *Rejoice greatly, O daughter of Zion; shout, O daughter of Jerusalem: behold, thy King cometh unto thee...*[773]

57. Joseph was accompanied by two criminals; one would live and one would perish. Likewise, Jesus was accompanied by two criminals. One would live, and the other would die. This fulfilled the words of the prophet saying, *he was numbered with the transgressors; and he bare the sin of many, and made intercession for the transgressors.*[774]

58. They taunted Jesus while He hung upon the Cross, fulfilling the words of the psalmist saying, *All they that see me laugh me to scorn: they shoot out the lip, they shake the head, [saying], He trusted on the LORD [that] he would deliver him: let him deliver him, seeing he delighted in him.*[775]

59. Satan caused them to say, *He trusted in God; let him deliver him now, if he will have him: for he said, I am the Son of God.*[776]

60. Just before Christ's death He cried out to the Lord as it is written saying, *And about the ninth hour Jesus cried with a loud voice, saying, Eli, Eli, lama sabachthani? that is to say, My God, my God, why hast thou forsaken me?* These

---

[772] Exodus 17:10-12.

[773] Zechariah 9:9;

[774] Isaiah 53:12.

[775] Psalm 22:7, 8.

[776] Matthew 27:43.

words fulfilled the words of the psalmist saying, *My God, my God, why hast thou forsaken me?*[777]

61. When Christ prayed, He was given strength, and *knowing that all things were now accomplished, that the scripture might be fulfilled...He said, It is finished...*[778] Jesus destroyed the House of Satan by destroying his two pillars of sin and death. Likewise, when Samson prayed, he was strengthened and he destroyed the House of Dagon.

62. None of Christ's bones were broken that the foreshadow of the Passover Lamb of Egypt would be fulfilled. *Neither shall ye break a bone thereof.*[779] *He keepeth all his bones: not one of them is broken.*[780]

63. At Christ's death the graves were opened and at His resurrection the dead were raised[781] fulfilling the words of the prophet saying, *Thy dead [men] shall live, [together with] my dead body shall they arise. Awake and sing, ye that dwell in dust: for thy dew [is as] the dew of herbs, and the earth shall cast out the dead.*[782]

64. At Christ's death He figuratively crossed over the Jordan with a supporting company. Likewise, David crossed the Jordan with his company.

65. At Christ's death He figuratively crossed over the Jordan with a supporting company. Likewise, Joshua crossed the Jordan with his company.

66. They pierced Christ's side[783] that the words of the prophet would be fulfilled saying, *they shall look upon me whom they have pierced, and they shall mourn for him, as one mourneth for [his] only [son], and shall be in bitterness for him, as one that is in bitterness for [his] firstborn.*[784]

---

[777] Psalm 22:1.
[778] John 19:28, 30.
[779] Exodus 12:46.
[780] Psalm 34:20.
[781] Matthew 27:51.
[782] Isaiah 26:19.
[783] John 19:34.
[784] Zechariah 12:10.

67. As it is written, *He made His grave with the wicked, and with the rich in His death.*[785]

68. Christ's confinement in the tomb was foreshadowed by Joseph in the prison house, Jonah in the belly of the fish, and Joseph in the pit without water.

69. They came to Joseph bearing spicery, balm and myrrh; an event that foreshadowed the women that came to the tomb to prepare Christ's body.

70. On the 15th of Nisan Jesus rested, sinless in the tomb on the Sabbath, while Israel celebrated the feast of Unleavened Bread which symbolized Christ, the Bread of Life that was without sin. The unleavened bread was pierced, striped, and bruised.

71. Before Christ's resurrection, two angels came to call Him forth. This was foreshadowed by the two messengers that came to give the GOOD NEWS to David.

72. Christ's resurrection was foreshadowed by the resurrection of Jonah from the fish, after three days and three nights.

73. Like David, at Christ's resurrection, both crossed back over Jordan. The first crossed literally, the second crossed supernaturally.

74. Like Daniel, the door to the tomb was rolled away, and both were brought out of the tomb of death.

75. The King was overjoyed that Daniel, like Jesus survived the night in the tomb.

76. Like Daniel, the tomb of Jesus was sealed.

77. Christ's empty tomb is a symbol of His resurrecting power, just as the tomb of Elisha resurrected the dead man.

78. Three days after the Passover, Israel celebrated the Feast of First Fruits. It is written, *But now is Christ risen from the dead, [and] become the firstfruits of them that slept.*[786]

79. After Christ was resurrected, He was given change of garments and He ascended to the throne. Likewise, Joseph was given change of garments and ascended from the prison house to the throne.

---

[785] Isaiah 53:9.
[786] 1 Corinthians 15:20.

80. Joseph became second in command of the Kingdom as a foreshadow of Christ's position as second in command in the Universe.

81. *As Jonas was three days and three nights in the whale's belly; so shall the Son of man be three days and three nights in the heart of the earth.*[787]

82. After Christ's resurrection, He spent 40 days preaching among the lost of Israel. Likewise, after the resurrection of Jonah from the great fish, Jonah preached 40 days among the lost of Nineveh. Both rescued many from death.

83. It is written that Samson killed more in death than in life. Likewise, Jesus continues to cause the death of the old man and the rebirth of the new in countless numbers.

84. Jesus serves as the judge of the Universe as foreshadowed by Solomon before Him.

85. All was fulfilled in accordance with the prophecy given to Daniel by Gabriel. Christ's death was on the very same day specified by the prophecy, three and a half years after His anointing by John. As it is written, *after threescore and two weeks shall Messiah be cut off, but not for himself: and the people of the prince that shall come shall destroy the city and the sanctuary; and the end thereof [shall be] with a flood, and unto the end of the war desolations are determined.*

86. After Christ's death, Jerusalem and the sanctuary were destroyed by the Romans in 70AD just as it is written in Daniel.

87. Fifty days after the Feast of Firstfruits, the people celebrated the Feast of Pentecost to commemorate the giving of the Law to Moses at Mount Sinai. The Feast of Pentecost foreshadowed the outpouring of the Holy Spirit on Christ's followers at Mount Zion as it is written, *And there appeared unto them cloven tongues like as of fire, and it sat upon each of them. And they were all filled with the Holy Ghost...*[788]

---

[787] Matthew 12:40. Jonah 1:17.
[788] Acts 2:3, 4.

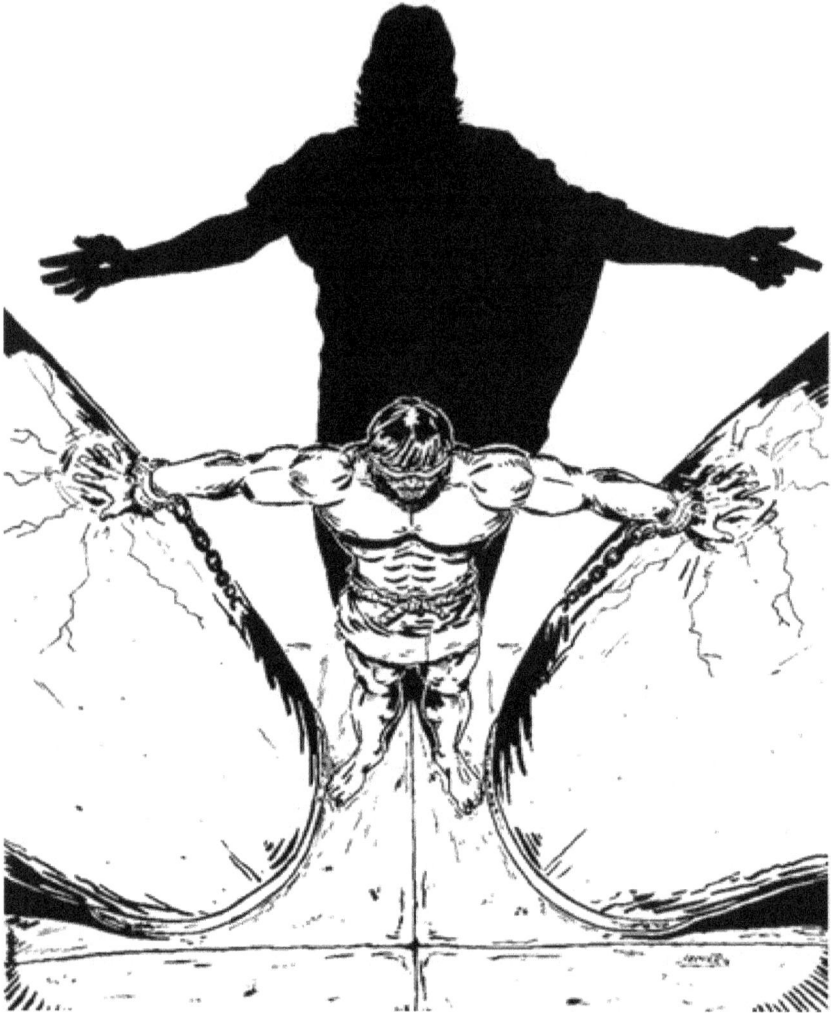

The evidence connecting events of Old Testament characters in the same order with events in the life of Christ is overwhelming and is far beyond coincidence. And the evidence shows that a Universe governed by Satan would be most miserable.

Jesus provides mankind a timeline of the events through the account of the Sanctuary that was given to Moses. It provides the path or road map of the Plan of Salvation, step by step. Likewise, the events in the accounts of the Guardians provide a sure timeline of the Plan of Salvation. On top of that, the prophecies, the chiastic structures, and the Helical Wave transforms add to the abundance of evidence. When truth is laid upon truth the interpretation is sure. *For precept [must be] upon precept, precept upon precept; line upon line, line upon line; here a little, [and] there a little*...[789] When these events are considered together, they reveal the time and events leading to the completion of the Plan of Salvation. And the final events have long been in motion.

There is a HARMONY OF THE SCRIPTURES that far transcends the HARMONY OF THE GOSPELS. The Old and New Testament are like identical twins in many ways, yet they independently and constructively support each other as a finely woven linen. And the Scriptures are as the Light of the World providing illumination, even as a finely woven COAT OF MANY COLORS.

---

[789] Isaiah 28:10.

19 *Angelic Messages: World Warned*

I saw another angel come down from heaven, having great power; and the earth was lightened with his glory... And I heard another voice from heaven, saying, Come out of her, my people, that ye be not partakers of her sins, and that ye receive not of her plagues. For her sins have reached unto heaven, and God hath remembered her iniquities.[790] And this gospel of the kingdom shall be preached in all the world for a witness unto all nations; and then shall the end come.[791]

Time will soon be no longer. The final warnings have already been given and the last events of Earth's history are rapidly coming to a close. At this very moment angel messengers are giving the last warnings[792] to the world of the soon coming judgments and the destruction of the earth. For it is written, *as it was in the days of Noe, so shall it be also in the days of the Son of man... and the flood came, and destroyed them all.*[793] All must make their decision now while there is still time *for in one hour is thy judgment come.*[794] For it is also written, *multitudes, multitudes in the valley of decision: for the day of the LORD [is] near in the valley of decision. The sun and the moon shall be darkened, and the stars shall withdraw their shining. The LORD also shall roar out of Zion, and utter his voice from Jerusalem; and the heavens and the earth shall shake: but the LORD [will be] the hope of his people, and the strength of the children of Israel.*[795]

---

[790] Revelation 18:1-5.
[791] Matthew 24:14.
[792] Revelation 18:
[793] Luke 17:26, 27.
[794] Revelation 18:10.
[795] Joel 3:14-16.

Satan and his forces continue to blind men that they may not see the hidden treasures of the WORD. Satan viciously destroys Christ's witnesses. Satan knows that without a Savior, mankind is doomed. Jesus empowered His apostles and disciples with the Holy Spirit[796] and they were filled with the light of the Word and the inspiration of the Spirit, and began to speak with other tongues. The people marveled at them wondering how they could speak in so many tongues. So Peter addressed them saying, ***this is that which was spoken by the prophet Joel; And it shall come to pass in the last days, saith God, I will pour out of my Spirit upon all flesh: and your sons and your daughters shall prophesy, and your young men shall see visions, and your old men shall dream dreams... The sun shall be turned into darkness, and the moon into blood, before that great and notable day of the Lord come: And it shall come to pass, [that] whosoever shall call on the name of the Lord shall be saved.***[797]

Many travelers from far distant lands heard the words of Christ's witnesses and returned to their own lands with the Good News. You might say Christ's apostles and disciples set the world on fire with the illumination of the Spirit, but soon thereafter, Satan set out to destroy them. Christ's messengers spread the WORD to the four corners of the then known world, in keeping with the Great Commission that Jesus gave them. Afterwards they were martyred by the works of Satan and his demons.

But this in and of itself provides great evidence of Christ's resurrection. What the martyrs saw and touched convinced them that Jesus is the Messiah and the Way, the Truth, and the Life. They were transformed from their cowardice to their willingness to be martyred because they were absolutely convinced that Jesus was the Messiah. And many of them sit in judgment in Heaven's Court today bearing witness of the heinous acts that brought about their premature deaths. Peter was crucified upside down. Philip was scourged, imprisoned and crucified. James the son of Zebedee was beheaded. Andrew the brother of Peter was tied to the Cross

---

[796] Acts 2:4.
[797] Acts 2:14-21.

and endured a long miserable death. Thomas was run through with a spear. Matthew was stabbed in the back. James was beaten, stoned and clubbed to death. Jude was crucified. Simon the Canaanite was crucified. Bartholomew was beaten and crucified. Luke was hanged on an olive tree. Paul was beheaded. And Stephen was stoned to death. And there are many more. [798]

Mankind can no more destroy Christ's two witnesses[799] than cleanse himself of his own sins. One witness is the Old wherein Jesus was concealed among the writings of Moses, and the prophets, and the psalmist. The other witness is the New, the writings of Christ's apostles and disciples wherein Jesus is revealed. Though mankind destroyed Christ's two witnesses in the streets, burning the Scriptures with fire, they were restored to life that they might complete the mission. For *this gospel of the kingdom shall be preached in all the world for a witness unto all nations; and then shall the end come.*[800] *Behold, the days come, saith the Lord GOD, that I will send a famine in the land, not a famine of bread, nor a thirst for water, but of hearing the words of the LORD: And they shall wander from sea to sea, and from the north even to the east, they shall run to and fro to seek the word of the LORD, and shall not find [it].*[801] And the end time is fast approaching.

The final verdict will soon be reached and the judgments will be delivered. Study the Scriptures before it becomes too late.

---

[798] Foxe, J., and Berry, W.G. (1900). Foxe's Book of Martyrs. London, The Religious Tract Society.
[799] Revelation 11:3.
[800] Matthew 24:14.
[801] Amos 8:11, 12.

20 *Court Deliberations*

And at that time shall Michael stand up, the great prince which standeth for the children of thy people: and there shall be a time of trouble, such as never was since there was a nation [even] to that same time: and at that time thy people shall be delivered, every one that shall be found written in the book. And many of them that sleep in the dust of the earth shall awake, some to everlasting life, and some to shame [and] everlasting contempt... But thou O Daniel shut up the words, and seal the book, [even] to the time of the end...[802]

Satan's time is almost up. He now goes around like a roaring lion, seeking who he might destroy. Jesus said of Satan, *Thou [wast] perfect in thy ways from the day that thou wast created, till iniquity was found in thee. By the multitude of thy merchandise they have filled the midst of thee with violence, and thou hast sinned: therefore I will cast thee as profane out of the mountain of God: and I will destroy thee, O covering cherub...*[803] But before Satan's case is decided, his greatest treachery will be brought before the Court. Satan has led many among God's Creation to believe that the Ten Commandments were nailed to the Cross along with the ceremonial laws. By this single evil deception, countless men and women will be lost eternally. For Jesus said, *think not that I am come to destroy the law, or the prophets: I am not come to destroy, but to fulfil. For verily I say unto you, Till heaven and earth pass, one jot or one tittle shall in no wise pass from the law, till all be fulfilled. Whosoever therefore shall break one of these least commandments, and shall teach men so, he shall be called the least in the kingdom of heaven.* And Satan is the one that perpetrated the lie. Satan sought every means to destroy God the Father, so that he could rise above the throne. It is written that Satan was furious *with the*

---

[802] Daniel 12:1-4.
[803] Ezekiel 28:15, 16.

woman and went to make war with the remnant of her seed,
<u>*which keep the commandments of God*</u>, *and have the testimony*
of Jesus Christ.[804]   What did Satan attack?   He attacked the
Commandments of God!   Who does Satan attack?   He attacks
those who have the faith of Jesus.   But despite Satan's efforts, a
remnant remains that keep the Commandments and testify of Jesus.

God's LAW is a reflection of His character.   If He could have
changed His LAW, there would have been no need for Christ's
sacrifice.   However, like God Himself, the LAW is immutable.   If
it were to be changed or compromised in any way, then error
would creep in as Satan would have it.   And if it were changed, the
God that governs the Universe would be destroyed.   Likewise, if
several of the pillars of God's natural laws were to change, even in
the minutest detail, the Universe itself would be destroyed.   God is
unchanging, timeless, and undeviating in TRUTH and so is His
LAW.   The LAW has never been done away with.   No decree has
ever been issued by Christ or His apostles to change the LAW
before or after His ascension.   Changes to the LAW have been
instituted by mankind's religious systems, through which Satan
works.   These changes were instigated by Satan.

Satan's case shall soon be decided and then shall the door to
Heaven's Court be closed.   And we stand at the threshold of the
Door; we stand at a time when the Door to the Ark in the Court of
Heaven will soon be closed.   And the same hand that shut the door
to Noah's Ark will soon shut the Door to this Court wherein is the
Ark of the Covenant.   From that time forward, none will be able to
pass in front of the Ark of the Covenant.   The same was prefigured
by the crossing of the Jordan.   When all the people crossed over
the Jordan, they crossed in front of the Ark of the Covenant.   And
each that passed in front of the Ark passed over clean.   When the
Ark of the Covenant was carried from the midst of the Jordan to
the other side, the hand of God allowed the Way across the Jordan
to close, just as the veil to the Holiest Place will soon be closed.   In
the end, all the people of Jericho watched as the Ark circled them.

---

[804] Revelation 12:17.

In our deliberations we find that God is innocent of all of Satan's accusations. These false accusations and the crimes committed by Satan and his followers will be turned upon Satan's head. It is Satan that caused a third of the angels of heaven to fall. It is Satan that caused the death of the first parents by his devilish lie. It is Satan that caused evil to so consume mankind that God had to destroy the world with a Flood, that a few might live. It is Satan that continuously attempted to murder the Deliverer of Israel, the Seed of the Promise. It is Satan that tried to get Christ to fall to His lies during the Temptation. It is Satan that blinded the Pharisees, Sadducees, and the priests of the Hebrew Nation, the very ones that were entrusted with the sacred scrolls. Satan so blinded them that they didn't recognize Jesus. It is Satan that entered Peter as a ruse to catch Jesus off guard. It is Satan that has brought about endless wars through the history of the world. It is Satan that martyred untold thousands of the Saints. It is Satan that caused mankind to violate every commandment of the LAW that God gave Moses. It is Satan that tried to do away with God's LAW altogether, by lying that it was nailed to the Cross. It was Satan that would *speak [great] words against the most High... and think to change times and laws...*[805] Therefore, it is written, *I call heaven and earth to record this day against you...*[806] The evidence has been brought by the testimonies of the Two Witnesses and a Great Cloud of witnesses.

Choose you this day whom ye will serve; Satan *which your fathers served* or the One sitting upon the throne. The choice is yours. The testimony will soon be *weighed in the balance.*[807]

---

[805] Daniel 7:25.
[806] Deuteronomy 30:19.
[807] Daniel 5:27.

THE VERDICT

By the multitude of thy merchandise they have filled the midst of thee with violence, and thou hast sinned: therefore... I will destroy thee, O covering cherub.[808] Thou art weighed in the balances, and art found wanting.[809]

At the beginning of my journey, I assumed that the evidence would demonstrate that the Scriptures were authored by men; not God. How could an evolutionist justify the Scriptural accounts of a world-wide flood or Creation? The two appear to be at odds. I was initially convinced that the Scriptures would fail because of inconsistent and incongruent arguments by comparing literal accounts. That is, I fully expected to find that the logic in the New Testament would be contradicted by the literal patterns of the Old Testament. Instead, **the encoded patterns, waves, and event sequences prove that God exists as the Scriptures claim.**

Harmony of the Types is Proof

---

[808] Ezekiel 28:16.
[809] Daniel 5:27.

21   *Verdict and Judgment*

And I saw an angel come down from heaven, having the key of the bottomless pit and a great chain in his hand. And he laid hold on the dragon, that old serpent, which is the Devil, and Satan, and bound him a thousand years, And cast him into the bottomless pit, and shut him up, and set a seal upon him, that he should deceive the nations no more.[810]

S cenes of world history and the testimonies flashed before me in rapid succession as I continued to read the words of John and assemble the evidence. The world is coming into a time of an indescribable uproar, and soon will come a *time of trouble, such as never was since there was a nation.[811]* According to the prophet Daniel, *at that time thy people shall be delivered, every one that shall be found written in the book. And many of them that sleep in the dust of the earth shall awake, some to everlasting life, and some to shame [and] everlasting contempt.[812]*

The events surrounding the Second Coming of Jesus, by Daniel's prophecy will take place immediately after the books of heaven are closed and all cases have been determined, including your case and mine! Before those days, it will soon be commanded that those bearing the seals of God should not be harmed; *only those men which have not the seal of God in their foreheads*[813] shall be harmed. Trumpet after trumpet will sound as at Jericho. Something ominous will soon take place. I can hear the trumpets even now; can't you?

---

[810] Revelation 20:1-3.
[811] Daniel 12:1.
[812] Daniel 12:1, 2.
[813] Revelation 7:2, 3; 9:4.

When Christ's work is completed and all have passed before the Ark, the world will fall into two groups. Those with the seal of the Living God and those without. Those without are represented by the twelve rocks that were left in the River Jordan at the Crossing of Joshua and Israel. They will soon be eroded away and they will be remembered no more. Those that accept Christ as their Lord and Savior will Cross safely before the Ark and enter the Promised Land, symbolized by the monument of the twelve stones. These precious stones symbolize the spiritual Israel that is the Bride of Christ. Once Christ's review of each case is completed there will be no second chance. Jesus our High Priest will soon say, *Blessed [are] the dead which die in the Lord from henceforth: Yea, saith the Spirit, that they may rest from their labours; and their works do follow them.*[814] *He that is unjust, let him be unjust still: and he which is filthy, let him be filthy still: and he that is righteous, let him be righteous still: and he that is holy, let him be holy still. And, behold, I come quickly; and my reward [is] with me, to give every man according as his work shall be.*[815]

Once the work in Heaven's temple is completed the sins that have accumulated in the seven bowls will be placed upon the head of Satan, the scapegoat. John describes these events as follows: *And after that I looked, and, behold, the temple of the tabernacle of the testimony in heaven was opened: And the seven angels came out of the temple, having the seven plagues, clothed in pure and white linen, and having their breasts girded with golden girdles. And one of the four beasts gave unto the seven angels seven golden vials full of the wrath of God, who liveth for ever and ever. And the temple was filled with smoke from the glory of God, and from his power; and no man was able to enter into the temple, till the seven plagues of the seven angels were fulfilled.*[816]

And I saw heaven opened, and behold a white horse; and he that sat upon him [was] called Faithful and True, and in righteousness he doth judge and make war... And he [was]

---

[814] Revelation 14:13.
[815] Revelation 22:11, 12.
[816] Revelation 15:5-8.

clothed with a vesture dipped in blood: and his name is called The Word of God. And the armies [which were] in heaven followed him upon white horses, clothed in fine linen, white and clean... And he hath on [his] vesture and on his thigh a name written, KING OF KINGS, AND LORD OF LORDS. And I saw an angel standing in the sun; and he cried with a loud voice, saying to all the fowls that fly in the midst of heaven, Come and gather yourselves together unto the supper of the great God...[817]

And I saw an angel come down from heaven, having the key of the bottomless pit and a great chain in his hand. And he laid hold on the dragon, that old serpent, which is the Devil, and Satan, and bound him a thousand years, And cast him into the bottomless pit, and shut him up, and set a seal upon him, that he should deceive the nations no more, till the thousand years should be fulfilled: and after that he must be loosed a little season. And I saw thrones, and they sat upon them, and judgment was given unto them: and [I saw] the souls of them that were beheaded for the witness of Jesus, and for the word of God, and which had not worshipped the beast, neither his image, neither had received [his] mark upon their foreheads, or in their hands; and they lived and reigned with Christ a thousand years.[818]

Satan will be placed in solitary confinement until the end of the thousand years. And during those thousand years, he will have plenty of time to reflect on the great suffering and pain that he has caused. And he will have time to contemplate his own fate. Just like Haman, the plot that he had planned will come full circle and fall on his own head.

---

[817] Revelation 19:11-21.
[818] Revelation 20:1-4.

Epilogue: Great Cloud of Witnesses

Wherefore seeing we also are compassed about with so great a cloud of witnesses, let us lay aside every weight, and the sin which doth so easily beset [us], and let us run with patience the race that is set before us, Looking unto Jesus the author and finisher of [our] faith; who for the joy that was set before him endured the cross, despising the shame, and is set down at the right hand of the throne of God.[819]

The scriptures incorporate coded messages of the *mysteries of the kingdom of God*[820] *kept secret from the foundation of the world*[821] carefully concealed throughout Old Testament passages. The secrets are concealed that the enemies of the kingdom of heaven yet *seeing they might not see, and hearing they might not understand.*[822]   The hidden secrets provide an ingenious plan to defeat the greatest threat ever to confront the Kingdom of God. Since the *"Fall of Mankind"* the world has been caught up in a supernatural war between Christ and Satan.[823] It would have been easy for our omnipotent God to defeat a created being like Satan. But God had to defeat Satan with love, since God's character is love.[824] According to the Scriptures the plan to rescue mankind from sin and death would have been lost[825] should this encrypted evidence have fallen into the hands of the enemy. The pinnacle of the secret plan was predicated upon the victory of the Cross:

---

[819] Hebrews 12:1, 2.
[820] Luke 8:10.
[821] Matthew 13:34, 35.
[822] Luke 8:10.
[823] Revelation 12:7, 17.
[824] 1 John 4:7-16.
[825] 1 Corinthians 2:7, 8.

> *...we speak the wisdom of God in a mystery, [even] the hidden [wisdom], which God ordained before the world unto our glory: Which none of the princes of this world knew: <u>for had they known [it], they would not have crucified the Lord of glory.</u>*[826]

You see, we're told that if the plan were known by Satan and his forces, Christ would not have been crucified, and God's plan would have been foiled. Christ had to be crucified to rescue mankind. It was the ultimate proof of God's love and the ultimate proof that God cares. So the Scriptures had to be divinely encrypted[827] so that the forces of evil would be caught unaware. The unlocking of the coded messages of His death, burial, and resurrection had to be so compelling that there would be no doubt that God exists.

The coded messages kept secret since the foundation of the world were the hidden evidence that would vindicate God. Even though Christ gained the victory over sin and death at the Cross, Satan continues to war with God's people for their souls.[828] Satan is doing everything he can to blind the minds of men so they can't see the Truth. Satan and his forces have blinded the minds of men by the veil of disbelief. And he is working hard to cause those that follow Christ to fall. But God has provided a Way of escape hidden within the pages of the Scriptures.

> *... their minds were blinded: for until this day remaineth the same veil untaken away in the reading of the old testament; which [veil] is done away in Christ.*[829]

Yet, even unto this day, when the writings of Moses are read, the veil covers their hearts. All they need to do is turn to the Lord.

---

[826] 1 Corinthians 2:7, 8.
[827] Matthew 13:35
[828] Revelation 12:17.
[829] 2 Corinthians 3:14.

Nevertheless when it [the heart] shall turn to the Lord, the veil shall be taken away. Now the Lord is that Spirit: and where the Spirit of the Lord [is], there [is] liberty.[830]

The ancient Old Testament Scriptures hide a treasure map that provides the Way for us to gain freedom from sin and death. Once you find the golden keys and unlock the codes held by each Guardian, like Joseph, Isaac, David, Samson, Jonah, Elisha, Moses, Joshua and many others and compile the composite treasure[831] map, it will provide you infallible proof that God exists.

Conclusion

The use of scientific methods proves that there's a supernatural world that science hasn't accounted for and that very proof changes everything. Numerous lines of evidence are all internally consistent on an incredibly detailed and broad scale. We have touched upon chiastic structures, that like light waves, provide literary illumination that stretch from Genesis to Revelation. As if that weren't convincing enough, we explored the Helical Wave Transform that originates in Genesis and completes its revolution in the Book of Revelation. Then to our amazement, we discover that the earthly Sanctuary built by Moses at the direction of God, is a map of Israel through the wilderness, and it is a map pointing to the Sanctuary in Heaven where Jesus is working on our behalf.

Yet the Scriptures provide even more evidence. Based on the hidden code behind the accounts of our 7 Guardians we see detailed documentation of the earthly walk of Jesus from His birth to His ascension hundreds to over a thousand years in advance. More incredibly, the testimonies of the Guardians document the events of the present and future. How can you explain how the writers of the Old Testament documented detailed information about Jesus more than a thousand years in advance? Events connecting the Old and New Testaments are intentionally

---

[830] 2 Corinthians 3:16, 17.
[831] Matthew 13:44.

embedded and choreographed through symbolic encryption, so that the life records of Jesus Christ and the 7 Guardians, along with many other Old Testament characters, are positively linked as if by supernatural DNA. We can only conclude that a Being or Beings outside the realm of our time and space are communicating with mankind. I choose to call those Beings, God the Father, God the Son, and God the Holy Spirit.

What are the odds of these 52 events being so clearly connected? If you were to take two decks of cards and ask two individuals to select a card and place it down on the table and record it and then have each individual replace the card back in the deck, shuffle, and repeat the draw 52 times between them, what is the likelihood that the cards will be in order from one to 52? The number, in my estimation, might as well exceed finding a single atom out of all of the atoms in the observable universe! Scientists estimate that the number of atoms is on the order of 10^{87} or 10 followed by 87 zeroes. Suffice it to say it is an almost incomprehensibly big number because we are not talking about just one case. We are talking 7 independent Guardians drawing 52 cards in order. It is like finding a single subatomic particle among all the atoms of the universe. We can only conclude that the code that connects the lives of the 7 Guardians to Jesus was deliberately hidden. And the ties were made secret until after the work of Jesus was complete. We don't have to believe that nothing comes from nothing. Every step that Jesus took while he walked the Earth, from His birth to His resurrection and ascension was known more than a thousand years in advance in great detail. In speaking to the Jews, Jesus said *Search the scriptures; for in them ye think ye have eternal life: and they are they which testify of me.*[832] By this Jesus meant that the Jews thought their path to heaven was through their traditions. Jesus proved that even the traditions in the Scriptures were all about Him through the testimonies of His Guardians who testify that He is the only Way to eternal life. They are the Great Cloud of Witnesses![833]

---

[832] John 5:39.

ABOUT THE AUTHOR

Dr. Don Alexander served as lead geochemist in US NRC's Office of Nuclear Materials Safeguards and Security (NMSS) where he helped develop regulations for the disposition of Nuclear High Level Waste. He later worked for DOE's Office of Civilian Radioactive Waste Management (OCRWM), serving as a liaison to the Nuclear Energy Agency in Paris. At OCRWM, he managed the development of Site Characterization Plans for the evaluation of a U.S. National Repository. With DOE's Office of Energy Waste Management (EM), he led International Technology Program missions to the Former Soviet Union (FSU), Japan, France, England, Italy, Germany, Hungary, and throughout Europe. He led a mission to the FSU and established the first exchange of scientists working on nuclear waste programs between the United States Department of Energy's National Laboratories and the Former Soviet Union. In that capacity, he negotiated for the transfer of Russian data on the effects of radiation on workers and civilians in the Urals. Don taught for a number of years as a Clinical Professor in the Department of Environmental Health Sciences, Tulane University School of Public Health and Tropical Medicine and served as PhD Co-Chair for three dissertations.

Don holds a Doctorate of Philosophy in Geology, specializing in Geochemistry, from the University of Michigan.

Over the past twenty years Don and his wife JaNa have been searching the Scriptures together, compiling evidence of the existence of God. Don serves in a multicultural community. Don and JaNa have formed *Sword Bearers Ministries.*

---

[833] Hebrews 12:1.

Inside Back Cover: We stand at the threshold of the Door to the Mercy Seat where our sins can be forgiven; but we live at a time when the Door to the Ark in the Court of Heaven will soon be closed. And then the words of the Savior will ring out saying, *He that is unjust, let him be unjust still: and he which is filthy, let him be filthy still: and he that is righteous, let him be righteous still: and he that is holy, let him be holy still.*[834]

When all the people crossed over the Jordan, they crossed in front of the Ark of the Covenant. And each soul that passed in front of the Ark passed over clean. But once they passed through the "passage door" the Jordan was closed. From that point forward no one could pass over in front of the Ark.

And the same hand that shut the door to Noah's Ark will soon shut the Door to this Heavenly Court wherein is the Ark of the Covenant. From that time forward, none will be able to pass in front of the Ark of the Covenant.

---

[834] Revelation 22:11.